# THE HOUSE THAT BUILT ME

## JACKIE MCGREGOR

# THE HOUSE THAT BUILT ME

Edited and with an introductory chapter by

## JACKIE MCGREGOR

In loving memory of Chris and Jack McGregor

ISBN 9781783758821

This book is dedicated with love to:

Steven and Ben,

and to the miraculous Mr JC

*Each corner houses memories*

*Of lives that have passed through.*

**From the poem 'Waterloo'
by Jackie McGregor**

# Message of Support

*It's heartening to learn that you are doing all you can to help raise awareness about Alzheimer's disease.*

*Warmest wishes for every success with your book.*

HRH The Duchess of Cambridge.

# Contents

# ACKNOWLEDGEMENTS

Sincere thanks to the following people:

Hazel Cushion, Rebecca Lloyd, Anne Porter, Bethan James and all at Accent Press, big thanks for all your help, support and guidance and for taking this project on.

To each one of the celebrities who have contributed memories and photographs. Thank you for your support and kindness and for taking the time out of very busy schedules to contribute to this project. Also thanks to all of the managers, agents and PAs who made it possible, in particular, Michelle Wales.

To lovely Lorraine Kelly, thank you for your help and kindness.

Thank you to Paul Allen, Celebrity Liaison Officer for the Alzheimer's Society and also Rob Stewart, Alzheimer's Society Press Officer, for all your help.

Thanks also to the Alzheimer's Society for all the important work you do. Your Talking Point forum was invaluable to me.

To the mysterious Mr Moffat for his unexpected visit which resulted in the creation of this book.

To Sandra Chapman, whose friendship has been a wonderful gift. Thank you for everything Sandra.

To my forever friend, Heather Longwell. I will never forget your support at my father's funeral, Heather, it meant so much.

To Ann McKenna, who never gave up on our friendship when I was housebound, and kept the 'do' looking great throughout.

To Holly Morrison whose friendship, laughs, emergency walks and lifts helped me through the darkest days.

To Trisha Ashley and Milly Johnson, two wonderful authors and extremely kind ladies, your help and support has been much appreciated, thank you.

To the love of my life, Steven, and the light of my life, Ben, you're my boat and my helicopter. Thank you seems insufficient words for what you've both given me, but thank you anyway.

And last but never least, to my sweet Lord for the prayers answered and the one set of footprints. I dedicate this work to you for success and thank you for my blessings.

# GRIEF ENCOUNTER
## by Jackie McGregor

I live in a house filled with spectres, so it should have come as no surprise when a ghost hunter arrived at my door. I surveyed him with suspicion. I could tell that in his head an entire silent conversation was unfolding. He knew why he was there, his story was stored in his every cell, he was a memory card of his own history; he appeared to be waiting on my recognising him, though to me, he was simply a stranger. I waited in the doorway, feeling uneasy. Whatever he wanted I could tell he was hesitant about revealing the reason for his approach.

'I've come back!' he uttered, choking with emotion on the words.

'I'm sorry, I don't understand,' I replied, deciding the man was a bit barmy.

'I used to live here,' he said and sighed with immense sadness.

'I'm sorry, you must be mistaken. I've lived here my entire life, nearly fifty years!' I replied possessively.

'I moved to New Zealand twenty-five years ago,' he blurted out, 'but I lived here in this house from 1944 to 1964. There used to be a big tree here.' He pointed to the exact spot where indeed there had once stood a beautiful pink cherry-blossom tree.

'It came down in a storm when I was small,' I said. 'Its roots pulled up most of the concrete path when it fell. I was glad it was blown down – its branches used to make spooky shapes outside my window. They looked like a witch's gnarled hands, clawed over; it felt like they were coming to get me'.

I was startled by myself sharing this childhood secret with a stranger, but evidently he wasn't a stranger to the house. No one else would have remembered that tree; it had disappeared over forty years before.

'There used to be a scullery at the back of the house and a

1

wash house with a corrugated roof. I used to love listening to the rain hammering on it. There was a little sunroom at the side of the house, which led out to a rockery. Is it still there? My mother used to let me plant flowers there,' he smiled, and I could see that in his mind's eye he was back in his childhood again.

'No, the rockery has gone. The scullery, sunroom and wash house aren't there anymore either.' I got an odd feeling in my stomach as I realised he truly had been the previous occupier of the house.

'And the apple trees? My mother used to wrap apples in paper and put them in the attic until they were ready, then make jam with them.'

We both watched his hands as he mimicked his mother's apple-swaddling actions. I could see from his face he was feeling incredibly emotional. He was lost in his own world of remembrance. It was as though he was giving himself a guided tour of his past, reliving his life at the house. He didn't really need me there, his conversation was mostly with himself, it wasn't a two-way communication as he continued revisiting his yesterdays.

'Are the Bramley apple trees still there?' he asked, looking past me into the hall as if he was trying to catch a glimpse of someone or something familiar.

'No,' I replied, shaking my head. Did he really think that nothing would have changed in almost fifty years?

'My father cut all of the trees down many years ago, though my grandmother was a great fan of the Bramleys. She used to make jam with them, too,' and I felt a pang of grief. I hadn't spoken of my late grandmother to anyone in such a long time. I realised it had been twenty-five years since I'd seen her kindly face and watched her gather the apples in a wicker basket. I was a little annoyed that this stranger was evoking emotions I had kept tightly contained for what now seemed like an eternity.

I began to feel possessive of the house as I listened to the man. It was evident he was desperate to come inside for a look around, but I wasn't going to allow it. It felt a little as if my spouse's former lover had come back to try and rekindle their relationship. I wasn't going to invite this man inside to invade my privacy, my home, my world.

'My mother died. I'm back for her funeral. She passed away just two weeks short of her hundredth birthday', he confided in me. And even though this man was probably in his seventies, he suddenly looked like a lost, little, boy.

'I'm very sorry to hear that.' I said. My condolences were heartfelt because I too had not long lost a parent and inside me lurked a vulnerable, little girl desperately yearning to see her daddy's face once more.

'I lost my father three months ago,' I told him, 'though really I lost him before that. He had Alzheimer's, you see. Physically he was there, but mentally I don't know where he was. In the later stages the disease robbed him of his power of speech. I hadn't heard his voice for such a long time.' My own voice came out in a half sob.

He ignored my emotion and the information I had just imparted to him. He wasn't interested in my grief; why should he be? He had come here on a ghost hunt for his mother and his childhood. Why would he be interested in me and my heart that was as fragmented with loss as his own? We stood in memory-laden silence at the door of the home he still in some way regarded as his, two adult orphans united in grief.

'I used to take the tram at the top of the street to school.' He went on reminiscing to himself as he stretched his hand out towards the direction of the main road.

I wondered how, when he had been living on the other side of the world in New Zealand, his thoughts had turned to this house nestled in the side of the Cavehill mountain in Belfast. He would have been remembering this home with a different cast of characters, while my family and I had taken over the starring roles of the production that had played on in this house's stage, long after the cast of characters in his life story had taken their last curtain call. The house may have played a part in his life history for twenty years but it had been the theatre for my entire life's production to date. My occupancy had been more than double the years of his inhabitancy. I wondered, did the house recognise him? I experienced that familiar feeling of someone else being present, as though an invisible force was watching us.

Sometimes I feel as though this house has a heartbeat and a spirit of its own. I spend long periods of quiet here while I write, in solitude, but rather than feeling alone, it's as though a very good friend is sitting there in comfortable silence with me, reading over my shoulder, scrutinising my words. This home contains the invisible footprints where my adored family once walked. The mirrors here have reflected back the image of every face I have ever loved. My beloved, late parents have left a whisper of their souls behind in the rooms. Within these walls I became a daughter, a grandchild, a sister, an aunt, a niece, a woman, a writer, a wife, a mother, an orphan; this place is so much more than just bricks and mortar. This is the house that built me.

# R. J. ELLORY

*R. J. Ellory is a writer, born in Birmingham, England. He has written
fourteen critically acclaimed novels to date.*

We knew there were ghosts, of course. There was never any
doubt in our minds. Ever since our mother died, my brother and I
slept in her room and we wondered if she was there too.

It was an old house; built in 1832, it had a plaque on the
garden wall giving the date and the name of the architect. In the
cellar there was a walled-up door behind the stairs, and we
imagined that a passageway travelled all the way beneath Old
Yardley to the village church. We wondered if people had been
bricked up inside, never to be found again. They were haunting
the old house too, no doubt about it. Sometimes, lying there in
the cool half-light of nascent dawn, we could hear them
whispering in the walls.

But it was not the ghosts that troubled me. My concern was in
the bathroom. That room was long and narrow, and halfway
along it was the airing cupboard. The toilet and the sink were at
the far end, and you had to pass the airing cupboard to reach
them. The door to the airing cupboard did not close. The catch
was broken, and it swung ajar and stayed open just two or three
inches. Something lived in there. You could not see it, you could
not hear it, but down beneath the boiler it lurked and listened.

Seven years old. I would wake in the middle of the night and
lie there desperate to use the toilet. I'd drunk too much R.
White's lemonade, as was always the case, and I needed to pee. I
lay there knowing that I would never get back to sleep until I
went to the bathroom. And so I rose slowly, cautiously, the night
chill and quiet. Not a sound in the house but the creaking and
whispering of old wood, the settling of the building as
temperatures changed. Out of my room and onto the landing, the

carpet softening my barefoot steps, and I crept, crept, crept along towards the bathroom. Down three steps, my feet pressed against the edges to stop them creaking, and then I finally reach the bathroom door.

I pushed it open as slowly as I could. I could see the toilet at the far end. I had to make it all the way down there without awakening the boiler beast. He slumbered, but he slumbered with one lid open, his ears attuned to the slightest sound ... especially the sound of small children as they tried so very hard not to make a sound.

All the way to the sink, the toilet itself, up on the balls of my feet, knowing where to step, where not to step, knowing that a single wrong move would be my undoing.

Holding my breath, aiming for the sides of the toilet bowl, willing the water to make not even the slightest whisper. And then I am done ... and the moment of truth arrives. I have to reach up and pull the chain. The chain itself will creak, the lever clanking against the metal cistern, and the toilet will flush. That sound will wake the beast. There is no chance of the beast ever sleeping through such a racket. And so that is the challenge ... pulling the chain as smartly and swiftly as I can, and then turning and running as if the very Devil himself was snapping at my heels, the hounds of Hell behind him, their red jaws slavering, the white teeth bared, their eyes fierce and yellow and terrifying.

Every night I ran the gauntlet of the boiler beast, and every time I outran him I knew he grew meaner and faster and more determined to catch me. The simple fact that I am alive to write this today means that I was always a mite quicker than the beast.

But that house still stands, and the beast is still hungry, and I wonder what other little child tiptoes along the same landing – oblivious to ghosts and spectres, oblivious to paranormal presences and poltergeists – but all too aware of the boiler beast and the speed with which a little boy can be devoured if that little boy is not oh, so fleet of foot.

# KACEY AINSWORTH

*Kacey Ainsworth is an actress. She has appeared in many TV productions including* The Bill *and* A Touch of Frost, *but is best known for playing the long-suffering Little Mo in* Eastenders.

It's summer 1973 and our family is on the move outwards and upwards! We depart London and move up the social ladder.

Our tiny, inner-city, old, cold, bog-in-the-garden end of terrace is replaced by a brand new 1970s detached (by about five inches) three-bedroomed house. Our new home was on an equally new 1970s estate which bore an uncanny resemblance to the residences of Stepford.

The house was bang on trend with an open-plan lounge/diner and pine-effect wood panelling everywhere. We also had an olive green and white Formica kitchen and an avocado suite in the bathroom.

As the removal men lugged boxes to and fro, my mother was tripping over her flared trousers and getting her bubble perm in a twist trying to direct the traffic. My sister and I were told to sit on the roll of new bathroom carpet and not to move. Being of a curious nature, I inspected the Swiss-roll end of the new carpet and, to my utter delight, found it was purple and hairy just like the fur on a *Sesame Street* character! The thrill of having a purple, polyester, furry carpet in the bathroom made me feel like we had arrived; it was also the start of a decade of static electric shocks for anyone using the lavatory!

*Kacey Ainsworth as a child*

# FELICITY KENDAL CBE

*Felicity Kendal is an actress who has appeared in numerous stage and screen productions. She is best known for her role as Barbara Good in the much-loved classic television series* The Good Life. *Felicity was born in Olton, Solihull, and brought up in India. She was made a Commander of the Order of the British Empire in 1995.*

I grew up in India. My parents never owned a home; we lived in hotels, guesthouses and hostels. Our family were never in the same place for longer than a few weeks. One week our home would be in a fabulous hotel, the next we'd be living in the poorest of hostels or a tea planter's house in the hills. It was a magical childhood, full of adventure and change. My father always considered owning a house to be a burden; he never did own any property. Even in old age, he preferred to travel the world and be as free of possessions as possible.

The whole of India was my childhood home and I can't remember ever feeling anything but safe, secure and happy.

# GEMMA JONES

*Gemma Jones is actress on both stage and screen. Her film appearances include* Sense and Sensibility, Bridget Jones's Diary *and Woody Allen's* You Will Meet a Tall Dark Stranger. *She won the 2015 BAFTA TV Award for Best Supporting Actress for her role in the BBC TV film* Marvellous. *Gemma was born in Marylebone, London.*

We lived in a tall, thin, upside-down house in a London square. The kitchen was at the top of our home and we grandly called it 'the nursery'. There was a coal-burning stove in the kitchen and my brother's cot was kept there.

I remember my mother returning home with my new baby brother. I recall very clearly walking into the room to welcome him home and seeing my mother sitting with the baby in her arms. What I don't remember, however, is apparently saying:

'Go away, I can't see you. You are not there!' to my new baby sibling.

Our house was number 22; it had lavender-coloured wisteria creeping around the first-floor balconies and a cherry tree in the front garden. The house survived the bombings of the Second World War. I was told that I spent many hours in the basement during this time, where my carry cot was put under a table for safety.

We had a happy childhood in that house until rising rents moved us downmarket when I was in my teens.

I occasionally walk past our old home now and I'm overcome with nostalgia. I recall the pea-soup fogs when we could barely see the houses opposite, and the horse-drawn milk cart trundling by. But my most enduring memory of all is hearing my father playing the piano as I came home from school during those childhood days.

# CAREY MULLIGAN

*Carey Mulligan is an actress. She was born in London, England, and grew up in Germany and England. Carey has starred in many productions both in the theatre and on screen, including the movies* The Great Gatsby *and* Suffragette, *and the play* Skylight. *She is an Ambassador for the Alzheimer's Society.*

My childhood home was a hotel. My father was a hotel manager and we used to live in the apartment on the hotel's top floor.

I remember every year there would be an *enormous* Christmas tree in the lobby. I was mesmerised by this tree, which glittered with lights and groaned with colourful decorations; it looked amazing! I felt like it was our tree and that all the hotel guests were guests at our family Christmas.

When it came to having fun, the hotel's laundry was our playground. We would ride the laundry trolleys as the maids cleared the rooms, and then we'd scavenge for left-behind trinkets after the guests checked out.

Living in a hotel seemed normal to me. When we finally moved into a real house when I was eight years old, I couldn't understand why we didn't need a key card to open the doors!

# VERITY RUSHWORTH

*Verity Rushworth is an actress best known for her role as Donna Windsor in* Emmerdale. *She has played roles both on television and in theatre, including recently starring as Holly Golightly in the musical stage version of* Breakfast at Tiffany's. *Verity was born in Bradford, England.*

Tottering around my bedroom in Mum's high heels, pushing dolly in her pram playing 'let's go shopping', has to be one of my fondest childhood memories of home. I would strategically place items on the chest of drawers to ponder over what to buy for hours on end: a comb, a Snoopy dog, anything. I remember being so eager to be a grown-up. After earning a much-needed five-minute break from playing shopping, I would run straight over to Mum and Dad's bed to watch myself jump up and down in front of the mirrored wardrobes. Looking back, it was rather a hectic schedule!

Being an only child, I would mostly play make-believe. I played a teacher, a doctor and a café owner; I took it very seriously indeed. However, please don't be fooled by the apparent sweet-natured little girl you may be imagining. A 'good as gold' child I most certainly was not. The mischievous side would catch me out eventually.

One Christmas Eve while raiding auntie Irene's make-up bag, an explosion of white face powder occurred. It went everywhere. The dressing table, the carpet and I were all covered in powder. When asked if I'd used the make-up, despite looking like a ghostly clown I responded 'No' with wide eyes and an air of confidence: an actress was born.

As I was growing up, we moved house a lot, so home for me was wherever Mum, Dad, Tiddles the cat and Nana were. Sleepovers at Nana's house were the best, mainly due to the fact she had real butter. Toast with real butter was such a treat; I can still taste it now. The sleeping arrangements were slightly unconventional, with me sleeping under a sunbed Nana had purchased, which hung from the ceiling above the spare bed, but I never questioned them. The most magical part of staying at Nana's was getting lost in her wardrobe of sequinned dresses. Since Nana worked as a jazz singer in the pubs and clubs, she had an extremely snazzy wardrobe; I was in my element trying on her gear.

Night time at Nana's involved putting PJs on, watching *Laurel and Hardy*, and usually the comforting sound of her whistling a happy tune of some sort. On occasion there may have been a cheeky McDonald's Happy Meal we'd have as our little secret treat.

Nana never saw me on stage professionally due to suffering from early onset Alzheimer's, but she did witness a particularly passionate Pocahontas, which I'm very grateful for. I like to think she watches me now, happy in the knowledge that she definitely played her part in influencing the profession I chose.

As I write this, I have a huge smile on my face reminiscing about all the fun memories I have of home.

# JO BRAND

*Jo Brand was born in Wandsworth, London. She is a comedian, writer and BAFTA award-winning actress. She is a frequent and well-loved face on our television screens, including appearances as guest host on* Have I Got News for You? *and as a judge on the ITV show* Splash!

I am blessed to have happy memories of a family home in Benenden, a sleepy corner of Kent. We moved there when I was seven or eight, and it was pretty much the perfect rural village setting for three fairly boisterous siblings looking for innocent trouble!

Life revolved around the village green: the church was at the top, the school was to one side, the vicarage opposite and, yes, there was a Post Office! There was also a sweet shop and pub. Our moral, educational and teeth-rotting requirements were complete.

Our house had a massive garden leading down to some woods and a stream where my brothers fished and we all consistently soaked and muddied ourselves, as play became an actual and painful reconstruction of a Native American massacre. When we weren't tormenting each other in the sultry, sunny days of the summer holidays, we'd tend to the needs of a small family of donkeys who continued to stare back mournfully, as we heaved and hurled bundles of grass for their delectation.

Our rural idyll didn't last forever but with huge affection I look back on those days and reflect on the fortune of our freedom. It really was lovely...

# DEBBIE MCGEE

*Debbie McGee is a television, radio and stage performer who is best known as the former assistant to her late husband, Paul Daniels. She is a former ballet dancer and artistic director of her own ballet company. Debbie was born in Kingston upon Thames, Surrey.*

My dad was an avid gardener and so had a big greenhouse. This was a source of great entertainment for my sister and I; we would make camps inside and it became our secret land. We would invite our friends into our camp, have picnics, and play during those lovely, long, lazy summer afternoons. There used to be a loose brick in the greenhouse, which my sister and I used to hide secret messages in. I often wonder if our little messages are still concealed in there now. I can't help but smile when I think back on those lovely childhood days; they were such happy times!

# SHANE RICHIE

*Shane Richie is an actor, comedian, singer and presenter. He is best known for his portrayal of the character Alfie Moon in* Eastenders. *He was born in Kensington, London.*

I've lived a surreal life; the ups and downs have been like a game of snakes and ladders. I've always remembered the early days of highs and lows. I have vivid first memories of my childhood home in London. Those memories consist of me and my large family sitting around a big table sharing, and sometimes fighting with siblings for, Mum's home cooking; it was simple but always substantial, delicious home cooking which we all loved.

Thank you, Mum, as I now know it wasn't easy!

# DANIEL BROCKLEBANK

*Daniel Brocklebank is an actor. He has appeared in numerous television shows, plays and movies including* Shakespeare in Love *for which he received a Screen Actors Guild Award. He is best known for his portrayal of Vicar Billy Mayhew in* Coronation Street. *He was born in Stratford-upon-Avon, Warwickshire.*

My childhood memories are filled with love, sunlight, lots of open space, animals, laughter, fresh air, horses and harvesting the fields.

I had a very happy rural childhood. I was brought up by loving parents who wanted only the best for my younger sister Sophie and I. My parents made sure we had everything we needed and often went without things for themselves to ensure this. It was a house filled with honesty, love and laughter and a place where practical jokes were always being played!

One of my earliest memories is related to a certain scent. Isn't it funny how a smell can transport you back to a place buried deep within your memory? The scent that reawakens those memories is freshly cut grass. We had a swing in our back garden, plonked right in the middle of our (what seemed at the time) ginormous lawn. The swing used to creak on the backwards swipe and I distinctly remember my dad mowing the lawn with a loud diesel-run mower. Up and down the garden Dad would go, wearing just a pair of cut-off jean shorts (well, it was the 1980s after all!) Back and forth, back and forth, I'd swing with the smell of fresh-cut grass in my nostrils, while the sound of the lawnmower and the creek of the swing filled my ears. It was the most free I have ever felt; it was that wonderful childhood freedom where everything feels like an adventure. If I imagined hard enough I could fly on that swing. I cannot smell freshly cut grass without being taken back to that memory of when I was four or maybe five years old.

I was never a particularly adventurous child; in fact, I was incredibly shy and timid. Though I remember urging myself to go as high as I could on the swing, and seeing the sun shining over the roof of the house if I got high enough. I would fall back down with butterflies filling my belly as I swung backwards, feeling huge relief that I'd not fallen off.

I count myself lucky to have been brought up by two such wonderful people, alongside a sibling I adore. Thinking on it, my childhood was about as perfect as a childhood can be. When I have children of my own I will do my very best to ensure that they have just as magical a time as I did.

# CARL FOGARTY MBE

*Carl Fogarty is a World Superbike race champion. He also won the 2014 series of* I'm a Celebrity Get Me Out of Here! *He was appointed Member of the Order of the British Empire in 1998. Carl was born in Blackburn, Lancashire.*

The house that has the fondest memories for me was the first house that my wife Michaela and I bought together. It was in a small village outside Blackburn called Tockholes.

It was called Chapels Farm and was a Grade-II listed building with five acres of land. We bought it in 1993, just after I'd signed with Ducati. The place was virtually derelict when we took it. Everyone swore the house was haunted, but I never experienced anything spooky. We moved there around the time I was becoming a well-known motorcycle racer and that brought its problems. In such a small village there was a lot of jealousy and I had a few complaints about how I was driving my Porsche down the lane. The council also got a bit upset when I built a tennis court without the proper planning permission. It developed into a right old battle and the local MP even became involved. But the tennis court stayed!

We put so much time and effort into doing that house up that it will always be a special place to me.

# DIANE KEEN

*Diane Keen is an actress who has appeared in long-running sitcoms
including* The Cuckoo Waltz, Rings on their Fingers *and* Shillingbury
Tales. *She has also starred in* Doctors *and on stage in* Vagina
Monologues. *Diane was born in London, England.*

The first home I can remember was a lovely, wooden, bungalow
built on stilts in a small town in Tanzania. I must have been
about three or four, I suppose, and my parents had emigrated to
Africa shortly after I was born. Although I was so young, I have
very vivid memories of that house. There were wooden steps up
to the wraparound porch, where my parents and their friends
would sit in the evenings, talking. They would also have
barbecues on the lawn in front of the house. This was the best
part of the day for me, as they would bring their own children
and we kids would play into the night, squirting each other with
the hose whenever we could persuade water to come out of it. It
was always a bit of a hit and miss affair with the water: it was a
precious commodity in the African bush and our games were
limited to a few minutes, as long as we were watering the lawn at
the same time!

I remember my room was large and airy with long, shuttered
windows on two sides. There was a big wooden wardrobe on one
wall which I used to hide in when my dad played hide and seek
with me. It never dawned on me that he pretended not to know
where I always hid! I loved bedtime and being tucked into bed
with my mosquito net by my mum or dad. Much to my dismay,
the walls were painted pale blue as apparently that was the only
colour available in the local store.

One thing I do remember was collecting the mica that was
lying on the top of the soil. It shone like gold in the sun and I
spent hours looking for big pieces that I could save in an old

Peek Frean's biscuit tin that my mum had given me to keep my 'treasures' in.

To me the house seemed enormous, although it probably wasn't that big; but it was always full of light, and lovely cooking smells coming from the kitchen, and there was always laughter.

There were big, old, slightly worn sofas and two armchairs in the sitting room and I loved to curl up on them in the afternoon, when it was unbearably hot, and feel the fan blowing on my face. My mum would read to me and teach me how to read the books myself. Once, my dad came home in the afternoon after work with a mechanical railway set and he and I set it up on my bedroom floor. I played with it for weeks and weeks until I think it broke, or it might have been put away because my mum was fed up with stepping over it all the time. I do remember coming back from nursery school one day to find it was packed away in its box.

I remember feeling very safe and happy in that house; and the nightly ritual of my parents sitting on the veranda chatting and watching the sunset, with me sitting on the knee of one or other of them, is a memory that has stayed with me all my life.

*Diane, aged four, with her father on the beach in Mombasa, Kenya.*

# SIMON WILLIAMS

*Simon Williams is a stage, screen and television actor best known for his role as James Bellamy in the classic TV series* Upstairs, Downstairs. *He has also penned two novels and several plays. He was born in Windsor, Berkshire.*

A poem about the angst of having to leave home for boarding school. First home then homesickness:

## 'Packing for Boarding School' by Simon Williams

Does she know what she's doing?
Packing me off to boarding school,
Sewing name tags on new clothes
Folding them into a trunk
(It belonged to Grandpa. What a comfort)
Vests, four, pants four – socks six?

Can't she see I'm sick at the thought
Of all that fun I'm going to have:
The adventure playground AND
A brand new science lab!
Does she imagine I really want
To be with boys my own age?
Pyjamas three, rugby shirts four.

The list allows new boys
To take their teddy bears for just a year.
(After that you're on your own, young man.)
'Mum, please shut up
About the larks Dad got up to
In the dorm before the war.'
Gym shoes, one. Wellington boots (winter only).

She's humming now as she puts spare laces
In an envelope marked 'spare laces'.
Her gaiety doesn't fool me.
She wraps a family photo in tissue paper:
The three of us, plus Monty, on the beach.
(Weren't we OK like that? Where did I go wrong?)
It will go on the locker beside my bed,
A glimpse of real life before lights out.
Home jam, one jar, face flannels two.

In goes my dressing gown from Peter Jones,
Red tartan, I can't think who I'm going to be
In all these brittle clothes or what to say.
Yes, yes I'll be as good as gold
Is that the deal?
I'm hollowed out with gloom.
'Twelve weeks isn't long, darling.'
She closes the lid – goodbye childhood.
Bible, one, Book of Common Prayer, one.

# CHERIE BLAIR CBE QC

*Cherie Blair, born in Bury, Lancashire, is a barrister and lecturer. She is married to the former Prime Minister, Tony Blair. Cherie Blair was appointed Commander of the Order of the British Empire in 2013 for services to women's issues and charity.*

*Cherie Blair, in her childhood home.*

My childhood home was a modest terraced house in Waterloo, Liverpool. I was brought there by my parents at six weeks old to live with my grandmother, while they carried on touring the country as actors. Apart from a period of nine months when my sister was born, I lived there throughout my childhood , only leaving at the age of eighteen to go to university in London. I can't think how we all managed to fit in, as the house had only two bedrooms and a small box room, and had to accommodate me, my grandparents, my great-grandmother and uncle and aunt. After my aunt moved out to get married, my mother and my sister moved in too.

When I was about eight, my uncle left to study drama in London and I became the lucky person who moved into the box room on my own. From then until I left home, I was the only person in the house who had a room all to themselves. Downstairs there was a back kitchen with a yard and a back sitting room with the TV and a coal fire which provided the hot water for the house. Once a week we would have a bath and my sister and I would sit in front of the fire in our nighties, drying our long hair. There was a best room – the front room – with my granddad's piano, and when he was home from the sea, the extended family would come round and we would all sing for entertainment, accompanied by him on the piano. My love of music and performing came from those days and remains with me still.

When I was studying for my A-levels my grandmother let me do my homework in the front room, which was a privilege. Before that I'd had to learn to study with the TV on in the background, which I think shaped my ability to shut off and concentrate whatever might be going on around me, a skill I still have.

The yard was small and backed onto the entry, which was a passageway between the sets of terraces and which we used to find spooky at night, it was so dark. As kids we tended to play in the street as, certainly until I was about ten, there was much less traffic on the road and children could all play quite safely. I can still remember the rag-and-bone man coming with his horse and cart every week calling 'bring out your iron' as he went along. At the end of our street were the shops and, from when I was about eight years old, I used to help my grandmother with the shopping. I had to learn by heart the shopping list and woe betide me if I got it wrong! I'm sure that's what gave me such a good memory and is the reason I can still remember our Co-op dividend number: 74101!

# KOO STARK

*Koo Stark was born in New York City, USA. She is a film actress, model and photographer, known for her relationship with Prince Andrew. Koo is a cancer survivor and campaigns to raise cancer awareness.*

A poem on the varied memories of my first home

### 'Stark Image' by Koo Stark

Home or house
Dog, cat, bird, and mouse
City siren, silent snow
New York City go go go
Music, flowers, fire aglow
Joy perfume, Broadway show
Doorman, chauffeur, private plane
Cardboard boxes with remains
*I Love Lucy* on the box
Tears spilt over missing socks
Sibling struggles
Maternal cuddles
Memories are in a muddle.

*Koo Stark, aged five, on her bike in the park in U.S.*

# PAULA LANE

*Paula Lane is an actress. She is best known for her role as Kylie Platt in* Coronation Street. *Paula was born in Hebden Bridge, West Yorkshire.*

My earliest childhood memory of home is of hay bales, hay bales and more hay bales!

As a child, I was lucky enough to live in the middle of a quaint set of cottages in a quiet village, surrounded by friends who were just a little younger than me. Most of our free time, in fact *all* of our free time, was spent outdoors.

The reason I can remember hay bales so vividly is partly due to the smell. We had endless hours of fun outside, jumping, hiding, even sunbathing! We were practically feral. It would be a shock if our bicycles were parked outside before tea time – yes, I'm a Yorkshire lass!

Home to me is tranquillity, seeing green, green grass and breathing in so deeply it fills every part of me. In fact, when I moved to London at nineteen years old, I had to make fortnightly visits home to do just that … breathe!

# KIM WILDE

*Kim Wilde is a singer, songwriter, author, television presenter, DJ and landscape gardener. In 1981 she received a Brit Award for Best British Female. She was born in Chiswick, London.*

We lived in a semi-detached house in south-east London during the 1960s. Our house was next door to my father's parents', who proudly named their side of the house 'Donna', after the big hit my father, Marty Wilde, had in the late 1950s. The next-door neighbours on the other side were called the Robinsons, and I recall my naughty and beautiful young mum, Joyce, singing the Simon and Garfunkel hit 'Mrs Robinson', while sticking her two fingers up!

Other childhood memories involving that house include the big freeze of 1963; blizzards bombarded the UK shortly after Christmas, and so began my lifelong love affair with the snow.

In the summer my brother and I would spend hours finding fun in the back garden; making rose-petal perfume from our grandparents' roses, bottled in glass Coke bottles to sell on the street in front of our house.

I remember well the night that man first stood on the moon in 1969; my mum, dad and my little brother Ricky and I watched this historic event wide-eyed on our tiny black-and-white television.

My favourite memories are of my dad singing and playing his guitar, as well as recording reel-to-reel stories for Ricky and I, speeded up to sound like cute Disney characters. Dad also wrote us a lullaby on an album called *Diversions*; it's the most beautiful song I've ever heard!

# LEMBIT OPIK

*Lembit Opik is a politician, author and broadcaster who served as a Liberal Democrat MP. He has appeared on several television shows including* I'm a Celebrity Get Me Out of Here! *Lembit was born in Bangor, Northern Ireland.*

We called it 'Bangor House'. Others knew it as '99 Clifton Road' – a name symmetrically befitting the gracious lines from a time when grandness was still admired, its formal majesty gazing down upon a rolling slope to where rocks separated Northern Irish land and sea. An example of semi-detached opulence, a great internal wall divided 97 from 99. I never saw the other side, and for simplicity conjured up a three-floor, mirror-image of our own.

The blessing of this home was due to the industry of my grandfather. His star-gazing genius enabled its purchase years before my birth, and we'd go at weekends, always with anticipation, as there was much for younger eyes to see. The cellars harboured fleeting hints of ghosts. Outhouses were etched with the ancient graffiti of bygone youth. In winter, northern winds tossed surf and salt against the rattling windows as the coal fire – agitated by the storm's angry draw – burned ferociously.

Next door was Bangor Yacht Club – a structure so self-confident it seemed to mock more modest modern residences around it. And so the two – the cube and club – sat side by side, an odd couple, never speaking, gazing endlessly across the Loch, counting the cycle of the tides.

With time, my grandparents went. The dancing fires, Christmases, pets and spirits departed with them too. Draughts alone were left behind to explore the empty rooms, while curtainless windows stared unlit and unblinking out to sea.

Developers saw their chance … since Bangor House was not for this new century (it stood on ground too good for equity).

I'm told new houses stand there now, but I will not look up to see them. I want nothing to tarnish my memory. In these alone there is a kind of immortality.

*Lembit Opik's childhood home, Bangor House*

# NICOLA STEPHENSON

*Nicola Stephenson is an actress who has appeared in many TV programmes including* Holby City, Waterloo Road *and* Emmerdale. *Nicola's on-air kiss with Anna Friel in* Brookside *made television history and was part of the London Olympics opening ceremony in 2012. Nicola was born in Oldham, Lancashire.*

I grew up in Oldham, Lancashire and, while we moved house a couple of times, the house I'd say I grew up in was two-bedroomed and semi-detached, where I lived from age seven until I was fourteen. It was on a fairly new-build housing estate, though you weren't allowed to call it that in our house. My mum would say, 'It's not an estate, it's a residential area.' I think there was a lot of that in the 1980s, people trying to social climb and appear more middle class and sophisticated.

The bathroom was downstairs and there were two bedrooms in the loft. We had a garage and smallish gardens front and back. There was a mushroom velvet sofa and brown velvet curtains. My mum was house proud but in a relaxed, homely way.

I was an only child but I never remember being bored or watching TV for hours. My parents were fun

*Nicola with her mum and dad, dressed in white for her First Communion*

41

and it was a very happy home. My school was round the corner, all the kids walked there together, without adults, and then after school we'd play outside, by the shops (where there was a fantastic chippy) or at each other's houses. That's something my children, growing up now in London, miss out on. 'Playing out' taught us how to socialise and be responsible for ourselves. I feel blessed to have grown up where I did.

Looking back, we may not have been rolling in money, but we had everything we needed and more. It was safe, and full of love.

# ANN WIDDECOMBE DSG

*Ann Widdecombe is a former politician, a novelist and columnist. She has made many television appearances, perhaps most memorably on* Strictly Come Dancing. *Born in Bath, Somerset, she was made a Dame of the Order of St Gregory the Great by Pope Benedict XVI for services to politics and public life in 2013.*

It would be quite difficult to say where I grew up. The answer always felt as if it should be 'everywhere'! My father worked for the Admiralty and so we moved about every two to three years. Home would one moment be a large, rambling official residence and the next a tiny cottage with two ponds and a delightful little stream with primroses on its banks. One house was so old that the chimney had steps where once the small sweeps used to climb; another had a mysterious room, locked up, where the landlady had stored all her children's toys and I could glimpse a large rocking horse through the keyhole.

So which of those many homes really stands out in my memories? I suppose it was the house in Singapore where we lived at the naval base between 1953 and 1956. There were banana trees in the garden and a large belt of bamboos at the back. An old disused air-raid shelter was supposed to be out of bounds on account of snakes, but I played there whenever I thought the grown-ups were not looking! The house was typically colonial and built on large concrete columns as a precaution against monsoon floods. It was there I made one of the longest friendships of my life – with the amah's daughter, Moi. We are in touch till this day and very occasionally cross the world to see each other.

For me it was a happy, adventurous time, but it must have been tough on my parents for the posting had meant my brother had to be left in England at public school for the entire period (oh, yes, that was actually normal then). My grandmother, who lived with us, had to be quartered on another relative for the duration. We had even had to find new homes for the dog and cat. At five, I was too young to appreciate all this upheaval, taking everything in my stride and enjoying it all. At the beginning I would ask my parents 'Where is Gran?' or 'When is Malcolm coming?' because I had some vague notion they would catch us up. My mother would reply 'one day', so I never had any inkling that we were to be apart for so long, and gradually I just took their absence for granted.

The reunion was joyful when we returned, and we all lived together once more in another house, from which we all moved again six months later!

# JANE McDONALD

*Jane McDonald is a singer, actress, media personality and
broadcaster, presenting shows including* Loose Women. *Jane was
selected by Lord Andrew Lloyd Webber to star as Grizabella in his
musical* Cats *in 2015. She was born in Wakefield, Yorkshire.*

My first memory is of a big house. We lived in that house until I
was seven years old. I remember it being very busy; it was a
boarding house and was run by my mother and grandmother.
There was a great deal of laughter due to my mother's infectious
giggle which always makes me smile. There was always the
smell of washing and ironing and, of course, food being
prepared. I used to watch my grandmother making the lightest
pastry for the pies (she also baked excellent cakes and scones)
while my mother prepared the sauces and meat, etc. They were a
dynamic duo who never stopped. I never really met any of the
residents; children (all three of us) were seen and not heard in
those days. My father was always working in the early days. He
worked down the pit and as a chimney sweep. He always had
black in his eyes from the coal (it looked like eyeliner) which
made him look even more handsome.

I was glad when we downsized and moved to a much smaller
house across town when I was seven years old. It felt like home
as soon as Mum and I went through the front door. There were
only enough bedrooms for our family and the meals being
cooked in the tiny kitchen were just for us. That was our family
home for the next twenty-eight years. Although it was a much
smaller house the happiest memories were created there.

*Above: Julie Peasgood*

# JULIE PEASGOOD

*Julie Peasgood is an actress, television presenter and author, born in Cleethorpes, Lincolnshire. She is best known for her role as Fran Pearson in* Brookside. *Her presenting work includes appearances on* The Alan Titchmarsh Show, Loose Women *and* This Morning.

I am five years old and my mum is washing me in our big tin bath in front of the gas fire. We are in the living room as we don't have a proper bathroom, and I love this Sunday evening ritual. I get to bathe first as I'm the youngest girl and I always have a little sneaky pee in the bath. It drives my sisters to distraction when they have to get in after me. This is one of the very few memories I have of our first house, 94 Newmarket Street, Grimsby – home to Syd and Pearl, four little Peasgoods and a population of cockroaches (or blackclocks as my parents called them). It was demolished not long after we left, but by then we'd moved up in the world to Scartho, a leafy, posh part of Grimsby.

Our cosy, comfy bungalow was on a corner, and Mum's garden won praise and admiration from all who saw it. Roses, dahlias, apples, rhubarb – Mum could persuade even the most reticent plants to flourish, and she invented recycling long before sustainability was a twinkle in any ecological eye. Her sweet peas were supported by old tights, our worn-out coats were cut up to make rag rugs and she encouraged my little brother and I to make everything our Ladybird books suggested.

Dad was a much-loved welfare officer on the docks and he brought delicious fresh fish home every week. He had the loudest whistle in town, so we always knew when he was near and I would rush out to greet him. He wrote poetry and would give away his last penny if needed.

I have so many good memories of life in that little bungalow:

doing handstands against the back wall and hearing ecstatic yells from the TV when England won the World Cup in 1966; Joey, our budgie, who could actually speak thanks to Mum's infinite patience teaching him; Dad teaching me to ride my bike (also displaying enormous patience) around our cul-de-sac; Jimmy Young on the radio and me swapping over to racy Radio Luxembourg; Mum pinning my Grade 1 ballet results on our Christmas tree as a surprise and the joy I felt seeing I'd passed with honours.

But my favourite times were in front of the fire with a cup of tea, a hot buttered crumpet and an Enid Blyton book, which I devoured as hungrily as the crumpet. I would dream of having all kinds of adventures, too, usually involving my best friend June, lots of chips and the amusement arcades at nearby Cleethorpes.

I would always look forward to returning home. Even when I left properly at sixteen to go to drama school in London, I would always relish going back up north for the holidays. I loved the smell of our home and that it was always bright, safe, warm and welcoming. Happy days!

# Dr Miriam Stoppard OBE

Dr Miriam Stoppard is a doctor, author, television presenter and advice columnist. She was born in Newcastle-upon-Tyne. Dr Stoppard was appointed Officer of the Order of the British Empire in 2010 for her services to healthcare and charity.

The first house that I remember with any clarity was in Bamburgh, a coastal village in Northumberland, where my mother, younger sister and I were billeted during the war. With the imminent threat of a German invasion we had been evacuated from Newcastle because we were Jewish. I must have been around three-and-a-half when we arrived there.

The house was set back off the road, semi-detached, surrounded on three sides by a garden, and a field beyond that was home to a herd of cows which my sister and I fed with grass cuttings after the lawn was mowed.

I remember the outside of the house very clearly. My mother used to say it was pebble-dashed but as a little girl who could go very close to look at the pebble dashing I realised they weren't pebbles at all. They were like pieces of glass that were smooth and shiny and reflected the sunlight. To me the house was studded with sparkling jewels.

Some pieces of the glass were so big that I could see my reflection in them and this gave the house a kind of mirrored magic. I was part of it, inside and out.

Our neighbour in the next house, Mrs Frater, I came to realise, was a keen gardener. Her flowers were always beautiful and because of her skill she was able, despite the inclement Northumbrian weather, to cultivate stocks in various pastel colours with their pungent whiff of cloves.

The smell of stocks is embedded in my brain, and whenever I see them for sale I buy them, so that I can bury my nose in them and be transported back to my pebble-dashed, war-time home.

Each morning from when I was five years old my mother would see me off for my walk to the village school. I now realise the distance was about one mile, but back then it seemed never-ending to my little, short legs. I recall those walks to school in all weathers, carrying my gas mask and a bag of cheese and onion sandwiches. None of the other school children could bear the smell of onions which meant that I invariably ate my lunch alone.

I've visited my Bamburgh house. It's a holiday home now. But the flowering fuchsia bushes which caught my attention on the way to and from school are still there, with their little ballerina flowers poking through the railings: the same bushes!

# AYKUT HILMI

*Aykut Hilmi is a stage, television and film actor, best known for playing Nico Papadopoulos in* EastEnders *and starring with Kiefer Sutherland in the American hit series* 24: Live Another Day. *He was born in London, England.*

We lived in a huge period house in north London overlooking a park.

My mum and dad were of Mediterranean descent and they worked incredibly hard to pay for the house. I loved being at home. I spent hours being creative and many more day-dreaming. I believed anything was possible as long as you worked hard and truly committed yourself to it. I used to love hearing my mum on the sewing machine at five in the morning. I remember getting out of bed to make a cup of tea to sit near her on those long, dark, winter mornings.

Christmas was always my favourite time, probably because during the year I wasn't given toys or gifts, so the thought that I would get a Christmas present was truly magical for me. I used to love placing the tacky decorations from Woolworths on the ceiling and hanging tinsel on the tree. It gave me so much hope. I remember sleeping on the couch and waiting for my mum to carry a large sack of presents to the tree in the early hours of Christmas Eve. I pretended to be asleep but would sneakily open one eye and watch her leave the gifts. I still relive those memories today, whenever I feel grown-up and trapped in everyday life; these memories take me back to those day-dreaming times and remind me of what's possible. To this day I am still a day-dreamer!

# ROWAN COLEMAN

*Rowan Coleman is an author who has published twelve novels to date. Her novel,* The Memory Book, *was a* Sunday Times *bestseller. She now lives in Hertfordshire.*

When I was about seven I saw Jesus' sandal go behind a cloud.

I was at school, in the playground. I think we were playing kiss chase; we usually were. And I saw it.

'Look!' I said to my friends. 'Look, Jesus' sandal just went behind a cloud!'

That was how I described it, although I should point out it wasn't just a sandal, his foot was in it, and I imagine it was attached to his leg, and then the rest of him. To me it was a fleeting glimpse of the great man, not a vision, but proof. Obviously the other kids scoffed, and when I went to tell my teacher she all but patted me on the head and then put me in the corner to draw pictures until home time. (I was an undiagnosed dyslexic; it was the 1970s, they gave up trying to teach me to write.)

Later that day, when I got home, I told my mum. She was very angry with me and sent me to my room. And I stayed there, peering out of the window at the clouds, wishing I could see an elbow or a lock of hair. Earlier that week we'd learnt about faith at Sunday school, and about how in ancient Rome the Christians had refused to deny their faith, no matter what anyone said, even though they got thrown to the lions, and how that was what faith meant. And I had seen that sandal. And I wasn't about to deny it. I saw Jesus' sandal, and I knew it in my heart.

Now when I look back on it, I can see it was my fledgling writer's imagination, or the way the clouds formed in a fleeting moment, perhaps an amalgamation of both. But the way that I *remember* it, the way I *feel* when I replay that moment in my mind is that it really happened, even though I know it can't have. Memories are the stories we want to tell ourselves about our lives. And sometimes those stories are magical.

# BOBBY BALL

*Bobby Ball is an actor and comedian, and one half of the double act Cannon and Ball. He has appeared on television in* Last of the Summer Wine, Heartbeat, I'm a Celebrity Get Me Out of Here! *and* Not Going Out. *Bobby was born in Oldham, Lancashire.*

I remember as a child living in a rundown old house high on the Pennines. There were five of us in the family: my mum and dad, my two sisters and me. We were what you'd call a poor family, but as a child I didn't notice that because the love that was in that old house covered everything. I grew up being loved and that stopped me noticing the poverty we lived in. I remember in the cold winter mornings after my dad had gone to work, my sisters my mother and I would walk down from the moors to the cotton mill where my mother worked, and we would be put in the nursery for the day. Then at night time, we would go home and have some tea. I would sit on my mum's knee in front of a roaring fire, while she told us stories of her youth. Sadly, those simple days have gone, but I still have my memories.

# EDWINA CURRIE

*Edwina Currie is a former politician, a writer and broadcaster. Edwina has also been a radio host and has appeared on numerous television programmes including* I'm A Celebrity Get Me Out of Here! *She was born in Liverpool, Lancashire.*

The first house I knew as home was in a cul-de-sac of eight houses called Meadow Way, off Meadow Lane, in the West Derby area of Liverpool.

It was at the very end of the tramline from town; I suspect that when my parents married, as the war ended, they took the tram out to the terminus, found some 'For Sale' signs, and decided to put down roots right there.

It was a modest semi, surrounded by green fields, nothing special, but for people who had grown up in the inner city, it must have been heaven.

I don't remember much about the house because we 'played out' nearly all the time. Photos show me as a small, curly-headed child with a cheeky grin; I must have been a bit of a handful even then. All the families in Meadow Way had children. It was a safe and happy play area, and we would head off into the fields with our little gang and come back filthy, me with my little brother in tow.

On one occasion my brother irritated me beyond endurance and I pushed him head first into the muddiest pond. Then I thought better of it and hauled him out by the straps of his little dungarees. He howled all the way home; I got a severe ticking off, and told to look after him better next time!

We had a lot of innocent fun, with our own May Queen every year – I was always an attendant, never the Queen myself. Birthday parties had everyone invited. I even had my own little boyfriend, John, who lived over the road.

The summer of 1951, however, brought tragedy. Our neighbour's daughter Gail came home with a bad headache, and ended up in an iron lung: polio. It was ages before she was well enough to leave hospital; from then on, she was in a wheelchair. A year or two later the Salk polio vaccine came in, but it was too late for her.

It upset my mum badly. She felt she was too far from her own parents, who still lived in a terraced house off Smithdown Road.

One afternoon Mum collected me from school and we headed off in the tram. But we got off a stop early, and there was our new house – slightly bigger, with an apple tree in the back garden, and a retired nurse living next door. And only the future ahead of us.

*Edwina, aged five, in her back garden with her then-boyfriend.*

# Sir Tony Robinson

*Sir Tony Robinson is an actor, author, comedian, television presenter and historian. He is best known for playing Baldrick in the television series* Blackadder *and for hosting* Time Team. *He is also the author of sixteen children's books and was born in Homerton, London.*

Mum and Dad were working class East Enders. Their ancestors had lived in Shoreditch, Bow and Dalston for over three hundred years. But Dad wanted to better himself. He won a place at London University, but couldn't go because my grandparents didn't have the money. Instead he joined the London County Council. He started at the bottom as an assistant in a workhouse, and ended up as Hackney's Assistant Education Officer.

He and Mum moved out of the East End and bought a little semi-detached house in South Woodford next to Epping Forest. He planted gooseberries, raspberries, blackcurrants, blackberries and pears in the back garden – all the fruit he couldn't get during the war. Our front door was always freshly painted, our doorstep always polished, our garden always neat and tidy. I was the centre of my parents' lives, and their love for me was exemplified by the way they kept our house and garden spruced up and friendly. Even today when someone mentions the word 'home' it's 14 Raymond Avenue that springs to mind.

*Sir Tony, aged four, on his first day of school
in the garden of 14 Raymond Avenue*

# MILLY JOHNSON

*Milly Johnson is the author of ten novels with over one million sales worldwide and is also a poet and newspaper columnist. Milly was born in Barnsley, South Yorkshire.*

The house that made me wasn't the one I grew up in as a child, but the one I 'grew up' in as an adult – and a parent.

When my marriage in Haworth was at an end, I wanted to come back to Barnsley to be near my parents as I had two children under two years old. A house came up for sale near to them which had been empty for a long time and, when I enquired, the price was incredibly doable. I made an appointment to see it and waited outside for the estate agent for over an hour but they didn't turn up. In that time, I had walked around it, looked in the windows, seen how massive the garden was – and fallen in love with it. Apparently the estate agent had been waiting at a much smaller house down the street which they thought I'd meant – no wonder it was so cheap, because they'd quoted me the price for that one. This lovely big house was out of my price bracket – but I wanted it so much. I put in a ridiculously low offer – and the owners accepted. I couldn't believe it.

Everyone who went into that house remarked on what a lovely atmosphere it had. We made it ours with paint, wallpaper, and extensions: a new kitchen, swanky bathroom, and an office covered in bee wallpaper. I wrote my first books in that house, through the night sustained by coffee and After Eights, and always felt – excuse the pun – as safe as houses in it. I sat on the stairs and sobbed with joy when I got my first book deal – happy memories. My divorce came through in that house (even happier memories), the children grew up in it; it was filled with cats and dogs and parties and fun. As I had such a long garden, mine was the one where our friends and their children came for the annual bonfire and the new-year parties. The house felt 'happy' that we were happy – and yes, I know that sounds mad. There was a benign presence in 'Longlawns' as we named it, though we never saw anything until the very last day we were in there. When I was chosen to do *Come Dine with Me*, that is the house where I was filmed – and yes, I won! And the house was a star – even the film crew said that it was one of the friendliest-feeling houses they had ever visited.

*The house that built Milly Johnson*

After fourteen years, we thought it was time for a change – something with fewer floors and less garden – and I was dreading having to sell it to someone who wouldn't love it like we did. Luckily the people who did buy it felt as if the house had picked them; they're as down to earth as they come and they were scared to admit they felt this way in case I'd think they were nuts. They have made it their own and their friends remark on what a lovely feeling the house has to it. And I sobbed my heart out saying goodbye – and thank you – to it.

On the last day we were in the house, I put down a pair of scissors on the dining table, turned around, turned back, and they had vanished. I couldn't explain it so I went into the kitchen to get another pair, returned to the dining room and the pair of scissors were back on the table with everything around them pushed back so I couldn't miss them. It was the only time I ever saw any evidence that something other than us dwelt in the house and I was delighted. I hadn't imagined it at all.

I now live in a new build and though the time was right for us to move into it, I do miss that extra-special presence our old house had. I pass it nearly every day and every time I do I smile at it. It was for us – and still is for others – very, very special.

# FEARNE COTTON

*Fearne Cotton is a television and radio presenter. She has presented a variety of TV shows including* Top of the Pops, *the* BBC Music Awards *and* Children in Need. *She was a Radio 1 presenter for ten years. Fearne was born in Northwood, London.*

My first memory of 'home' is of my dad, hammer in hand, covered in cement, building what would become my bedroom.

My first home was a bungalow in the suburbs of north-west London. My brother was about to be born and we were one bedroom short, so Dad got to work with my new exciting space. Being ever so handy, this was not a problem for my practical dad. He went about building me a bedroom which would protrude into our lovely green garden. My new baby brother would acquire my old room and my new build would be joined on to his. I was over the moon as I had a view of the garden from my window which provided hours of day-dreaming opportunities.

One birthday my dad, who is a signwriter, made a wooden Bugs Bunny birthday sign and put it in the middle of the lawn so I could see it from my window when I woke up that morning.

My room was full of My Little Ponies and Barbie dolls whose hair I would style/ruin.

Our little bungalow was cosy and often full of family and friends. I remember 1980s birthday parties, occupying the front room with caterpillar cakes and pass the parcel, and gorgeous summers spent in paddling pools in the garden.

I have fond memories of shouting over the garden fence to our Scottish neighbours, Joe and Lottie, who would let my brother and I sit in their car in their garage and pretend to drive.

Mum has many great photos of me, my brother Jamie and

cousin Biba, collecting worms and having adventures in our garden. My nan got me my first bike from the local skip and Dad fixed it up. The bike was pearlescent olive green, with a cream seat, and I would ride it around the garden for hours.

I haven't been back since we moved when I was around six, but I have very fond and vivid memories of that first place I called home.

# Deborah Moggach

*Deborah Moggach is an award-winning novelist and screenwriter. Her novel* These Foolish Things *was adapted into the movie* The Best Exotic Marigold Hotel. *Her script for the film* Pride and Prejudice, *which starred Keira Knightley, was nominated for a BAFTA award.*

My first home, where I lived until I was eleven, was a gothic cottage just outside Watford, right on a busy main road. Hardly the most romantic setting – but the house was magical, with gargoyles and turrets. Though surrounded by suburban streets, it was an oasis – it had a huge garden backing onto fields, and we kept a menagerie of rabbits and guinea pigs there. We also had a pony, Silver. Our primary school was right across the road, and we kept our pony in the field behind it and gave our friends rides at lunchtime. Needless to say, we were pretty popular. We even started a club devoted to teaching our friends how to persuade their parents to buy them a pony (needless to say, its hit rate was non-existent). Gradually the land became built over and Silver's field was swallowed up by houses.

Every day my father bicycled to work in London – ten miles there and ten miles back. He worked in publishing but started writing books himself, as did my mother; so he gave up the day job and the two of them sat side by side on the veranda, pounding away on their typewriters.

The sun was always shining, but that's childhood for you. In fact, the garden faced south and it *was* pretty sunny. Many, many years later I went back there and knocked on the door. The occupants took me into the garden which had been completely transformed – it was now a thick wood, and quite dark. But it was still magical, in a shadowy, brooding sort of way. And, of course, much smaller. The house was *tiny*. It seemed a palace at the time – but that, too, is childhood for you.

# CHRISTINA JONES

*Christina Jones is a successful novelist who also writes short stories
and articles for national magazines and newspapers. Christina was
born in Oxford, England.*

We – my mum and dad and I – moved into the prefab when I
was almost two. The prefabs – boxy, flat-roofed, detached
almost-bungalows, built as temporary accommodation after the
war for servicemen and their families – had been standing empty,
and were due to be demolished at any moment, but as a short-
term stop-gap my parents were simply delighted to have a roof
over their heads.

We moved in at the same time as all the other families:
twenty of them, all with young children, into twenty identical
prefabs on the outskirts of our Berkshire village. The prefabs
backed onto farmland and orchards, and overlooked a single-
track road, fields and trees, and vast stretches of shrubbery and
common. There were simply miles of playground and places to
explore, build camps, swing on ropes, splash in streams, have
picnics, play in hayfields in the summer, and slide about on tea
trays in snowy winters.

Heaven on earth.

I grew up in happy poverty, secure, loved and surrounded by
friends. All the adults were of the same age, ditto the children –
we had our own cosy little community. Therefore, as an only
child, I was never lonely: the two boys next door – Allan and
Paul – were my brothers; Shirley and Diane, on the other side,
were my sisters. And they still are.

We shared one another's homes, parties, outings; Christmases
and birthdays were riotous events with the whole street getting
together to celebrate. We had open doors – no one was ever
turned away. Good news and bad was shared by everyone, happy

times and sad were the same – no one was ever left alone to cope or struggle. Money was loaned and returned; clothes were shared; food was plentiful, because we all had very long gardens filled with vegetables and fruit trees, and many of the families kept chickens. There was always an abundance of fresh produce and eggs.

The prefab was wonderful: pretty luxurious for those days – with a small Rayburn in the living room which heated not only the whole house, but also the water and the towel rail in the surprisingly up-to-date bathroom. It also had built-in appliances in the kitchen, including a fridge – something I know my mum was extremely proud of – a copper boiler for doing the washing, a hob and oven, lots of cupboards, and a huge larder. The living room was always cosy in winter, thanks to the Rayburn, and lovely and cool in the summer, as it had dual-aspect windows which could be thrown open to catch the breeze from all angles.

There was a long passageway from the front door – with the lavatory and bathroom at one end, the airing cupboard (another one of my mum's joys!) halfway along, and two double bedrooms. We – the prefab children – all had the back bedroom, so we could lean out and chat and shout and laugh with one another along the row long after we were supposed to have gone to bed.

Year after year, the council sent letters saying the prefabs were going to be demolished and we would all be rehoused. Everyone grew very sombre on The Day of the Letters. Year after year, it didn't happen. We – the prefab families – grew up there, in our rural idyll (it really was). I passed my Eleven-Plus. Some of the others didn't, but it made no difference: whether we went to the grammar or the secondary modern, we were so entrenched in our companionship and extended family that nothing, educational segregation or anything else, could ever come between us.

We all had our first tentative teenage love affairs there; our first heartbreaks; some of us left school and found work, others went on to further education. The village grew around us – some of our childhood playgrounds became housing estates, some of the farmland disappeared to make a new road – but the companionship, the friendship, the happy security, never changed.

That house – that prefab – that temporary home gave me the warmth of a happy, cosy, loving childhood and coloured my life for almost seventeen years.

One the day The Letters came and they really meant it. The prefabs were being demolished to make way for new, up-to-date housing – and no, none of the prefab families would be offered one of the new houses. The street went into mourning. It was, without doubt, the saddest day any of us had ever experienced.

And the hammer fell quickly. Within six weeks we were all allocated new homes by the council – you didn't turn them down, you were told where you were going and that was that.

I still vividly remember standing in my bedroom as we packed everything away ready to leave, gazing out at the garden – the only garden I'd ever known – crying and feeling that my heart would never mend.

We were given a nice, new, brick-built semi-detached house a few streets away – the first time I'd ever had stairs – and we all hated it. Allan and Paul's family were moved to the bottom of the same road, Diane and Shirley's to the other side of the village. They all hated their new homes, too. Some of the other families were rehoused in the next village along.

It was awful.

Almost as awful as the day the bulldozers moved in and demolished our street, our homes, our memories, in a matter of moments. There was nothing left of the prefabs but dust and rubble. We all went to watch and we all cried.

So, yes, the prefab built me and my life. Everything I've ever learned was learned there, my whole life ethos is based on the prefab years. I still dream about it. In my dreams and in reality I can see it all as if I were still there: the rooms, the colours, the furniture, the décor, the garden: all of it. It's so vivid. I know if I was asked, I could recreate the entire place from memory.

Thankfully, I now write cosy, warm rom-com novels and the prefab, the street, the friendly, happy community and the pleasure of living simply with old-fashioned values, feature in some way in every single one. So in my head, that prefab – that temporary home that lasted for seventeen years – will never die.

# Lorraine Kelly OBE

*Lorraine Kelly was born in Gorbals, Glasgow. She is a television presenter, actress and journalist best known for presenting her daily morning show,* Lorraine. *Lorraine was appointed Officer of the Order of the British Empire in 2012 for her services to charity and the armed forces. In 2014 she received a Scottish BAFTA Award.*

*A young Lorraine on the streets of Glasgow*

I was born in Glasgow in 1959 and for the first couple of years of my life I lived in a 'single end' in the Gorbals. Pictured is me when I was young.

My mum and dad, Anne and John Kelly, were teenagers and one tiny room on the ground floor of a tenement in Ballater Street was all they could afford at the time.

My mum had the place shining like a palace and my dad worked really hard, putting in hours of overtime as a TV mechanic.

My mum had a tiny cooker and sink in one corner of the room and their bed was in a recess in the wall. We had to share an outside toilet with all the other residents in the tenement.

A lot of our family members, including my granny and granda Kelly and my dad's brother Billy and sisters Carol and Lydia, also lived in the Gorbals and it was a tight-knit community where people helped each other out.

When I was two, we moved to Swanston Street in Bridgeton to a room and kitchen with an inside toilet; but my mum still had to boil kettles for hot water and we all washed in the sink.

Once a week we went to the Ruby Street public baths for a

soak in one of the massive zinc tubs.

My mum made this house into a real home. It was warm, cosy and bright. I don't know how she managed to cook such brilliant, nourishing meals in that teeny kitchenette.

We had the first colour TV in our block and everyone came round to have a look at the 'Frank Sinatra special' that was being screened and to marvel that his eyes really were blue.

Our house was full of books and newspapers, and my mum and dad taught my brother and I to read and write before we went to primary school.

It was a happy upbringing and we wanted for nothing.

To make extra money for holidays and treats my mum took a part-time job as a sales assistant and my dad continued to work really long hours.

When I was twelve years old, our house in Glasgow was condemned and demolished and we were shipped out to the new town of East Kilbride where, for the first time, we had a house with a garden, a telephone, and a proper bathroom. I even had my own room.

I missed our old flat and all my pals and it's sad that all of the houses were knocked down and the communities scattered, but East Kilbride was a good place for a teenager. I made new friends and, when I left school, I got my big break on the *East Kilbride News*.

I was very lucky to have such a brilliant childhood and that's all down to the sheer, hard graft and loving care from my mum and dad.

# David Hamilton

*'Diddy' David Hamilton is a DJ and radio and television broadcaster. David has hosted over twelve thousand radio shows and more than a thousand TV shows, including* Top of the Pops. *He was born in Manchester, England.*

I was an evacuee during World War Two, but lucky to be evacuated to my grandfather's farm in Sussex. Tucked away in the Sussex countryside we saw little of the war. I just remember sunny days playing in the fields; it was a wonderful childhood.

On the farm was a very old cottage, dating back to the 1400s. In the grounds were trees that contained the most delicious apples. It was the former home of the miller who had run the nearby mill. I loved to play football in the meadows that surrounded it and to run with our black and white collie, Scamp.

When I was fifteen, my grandfather retired and the farm was sold. I was sure I would never return to the place where I grew up and had so many happy days. I didn't see the house for fifty years until I discovered an old friend was living there. My wife and I went to visit and spent a lovely afternoon in the garden with him and his wife. Seven years ago they moved on. I bought the old house and walked again through the fields I first discovered when I was a boy.

Though the nearby village had developed, little had changed on the farm. My grandparents died in the 1950s and my parents in the 1960s, but I often think how thrilled they would be to know that I returned to the place that they, for forty years and spanning two world wars, had called home.

# DAME MARY PETERS CH DBE

*Dame Mary Peters was born in Halewood, Lancashire. She is a former
athlete, who won a gold medal in the 1972 Summer Olympics in the
women's pentathlon as well as three gold medals and a silver medal in
the Commonwealth Games. She was appointed Dame Commander of
the Order of the British Empire in 2000 for her services to sport and to
the community in Northern Ireland.*

I was born in Halewood, Lancashire, in 1939, just before the
outbreak of the Second World War, in a newly built semi-
detached house with a front and a back garden. These gardens
were my father's pride and joy.

When I was a baby, I slept with my mother and older brother
beneath the dining-room table and behind the settee; this was to
shelter us from the bombings of the railway lines very nearby.
Our neighbour was killed by an explosion. Our windows were
broken by a bomb and I remember them being boarded up for
years. My brother vividly recalls when the sirens blared and we
were taken to the air-raid shelter.

As I grew up, I enjoyed the freedom of living in the country;
we had fields behind our house. It was a loving home. My father
was an insurance agent; he would travel around by motorbike
selling penny policies.

I loved school, though I only ever had average reports, but it
was always written on them 'is a very helpful, little girl!' I was
invited back to my school as a special guest when it celebrated
its seventieth anniversary, which was wonderful!

I was very competitive and tried to beat my brother John, who
was three years older than me, at every opportunity. We climbed
trees and ran through the fields with me shouting, 'Wait for me!'
after him. We played rounders with friends and I loved to collect
wildflowers.

My favourite outing was visiting a horse's rest and pet

cemetery about a mile's walk from my home. I also enjoyed going to visit my paternal grandparents who lived a four-mile bus ride away. We would call at the village swimming pool or playground on the way to my grandparents' house.

When I was about eight years old I had my first banana, which was a real luxury then; and I remember queuing for ages to buy a tin of peaches because food was rationed. I would often run errands for elderly neighbours.

I would go to school on the bus, which cost a penny, and then I would walk home, saving my return fare. I could then buy an Oxo cube or a packet of wafer biscuits with my saved bus fare, bliss!

I had a very active childhood surrounded by lots of love. I have blissful memories of growing up, they were happy days!

# BILL ODDIE OBE

*Bill Oddie is a writer, composer, musician, comedian, artist, ornithologist, conservationist and television presenter. Born in Rochdale, Lancashire, he is renowned for his nature programmes and for* The Goodies *which he co-wrote. In 2003 he was made an Officer of the Order of the British Empire for services to wildlife conservation.*

I was born in 1941 in Rochdale, Lancashire. In those days it was famous for being the home town of Gracie Fields and the Co-op. In recent years, it has had a rather less wholesome reputation as a hotbed of nauseating pederasty rings, but I certainly wasn't aware of anything like that when I was a little lad. In fact, like many people, I grew up in two houses – a cramped little terrace in Sparthbottom's Road (they don't name streets like that anymore!) and then a comparatively sumptuous semi-detached in Oak Tree Crescent in Quinton on the edge of Birmingham, which signified my father's climb up the accountancy ladder. (A skill, incidentally, that he totally failed to impart to me.)

Strictly speaking, I suppose the house in Oak Tree Crescent was home throughout my so-called 'formative years'. We moved there when I was about six years old, and I only officially left after I had moved on to university and subsequently to life in London. Nevertheless, it is Sparthbottom's Road that sticks in my mind and was the scene of my most graphic and maybe most traumatic and formative experiences. I suspect a psychiatrist would agree.

Most significantly, this was the house that my mother ran away from. Not that I can recall her ever being there. Presumably she was sometimes, but not ever as frequently as my dad, who conscientiously saw me off to school – six and seven year olds walked in those days!

He was always back for dinner which was prepared by my

*Bill Oddie with his father, on holiday in the Isle of Man*
*Mid-1940's*

ever-present granny who, in the absence of Mum, was, I suppose, the lady of the house, although frankly she lacked several of the skills post-war ladies were supposed to have. She could neither knit, sew, nor barely cook. Dad usually made dinner. Egg and chips. Always! Occasionally, it was augmented by Granny's contribution of a massive white bread sandwich spread with jam, condensed milk, or even sugar. To be honest, I didn't regard Granny with much affection, but two things she did provide; continuity and reliability. She was always there. Unlike my mother, who was rarely seen or spoken of. It was only when we moved to Birmingham that Dad told me Mum would not be moving with us. I was relieved, and it was not long after, that she was sectioned and admitted to a psychiatric hospital (no doubt referred to as an asylum) near Bromsgrove. All I had been told in Rochdale was that there was 'something wrong with her nerves', which I came to accept was a euphemism for 'unstable and sometimes violent', especially towards my father. I only once saw the evidence of this; I came back from school one day to find the kitchen strewn with smashed crockery, much of it spattered with blood. Granny was hiding, Dad was at the clinic, and Mum had gone wherever she went to.

I presume I sought the sanctuary of other local kids who were permanently 'playing out' in the alley. They were 'our gang', though 'playing out' could just as likely refer to kicking a ball as hurling stones at one another. I suppose they were my surrogate family. I had no siblings, and I recall neither friends nor neighbours! Where were those warm-hearted 'salt of the earth' *Coronation Street*-type people? Quite a few of them were away at war, I suppose. At the age of three or four, I understood nothing of that, but I do recall the ominous rumble of German bombers in the night and I knew how to put on a gas mask, albeit only in play. I was never aware of 'action' – death and destruction – but I do have an almost surreal memory of seeing a burning tank a mile or more away on the local moorland. As far as I am aware, enemy tanks never invaded Todmorden. Maybe it was one of ours. Or perhaps it was a dream.

Talking of sleep, I can still picture my bedroom. It was very gloomily lit (things tended to be during wartime) and the furniture was made of very dark, shiny wood. There was the odd vase or porcelain chamber pot, but no colourful posters or toys. It was less like a kid's room, more like Bates Motel!

As it happens, I did experience scary moments there. I may have gone to bed contentedly, but would sometimes be woken by the sound of voices downstairs. Mum had called in. With slight trepidation, I listened for a tetchy exchange of words between Mum and Dad, occasionally punctuated by Granny being told to 'keep out of it!'

Then came footsteps on the stairs, a door creaking open, and Mum kissing me goodnight. It makes me sad to say it, but I was not comforted, I was scared. I often pretended to be asleep and was left lying there trying to decipher the news on the kitchen wireless: a cultured but ominously morose voice talking of 'air raids and casualties' and warning of 'bombings and blitz'. To this day, I am unnerved by the sound of 'talk' radio left on, even though no one is listening. It reminds me of the war. That was scary!

But not half as scary as 'the night of the cat'. I have never liked cats, but after what happened that night it really isn't surprising. I don't remember if the animal had a name, or who had brought it into the house. It was big for a cat, white, fluffy, and nervous. A sort of ghost cat, if you will. I suspect it was no stranger to traumatic experiences itself since it spent much of its time scurrying under the table or hiding under chairs, a sign that it had probably had some kind of bad experience. Clearly the cat didn't like people and people didn't really like the cat much, especially me!

When bedtime came, I made absolutely certain that there was no cat sprawling on or lurking under my bed before asking Dad to close the door and make sure it was firmly on the latch. Only then could I sleep the sleep of the meow-less. But then came the night of the cat. It was well after midnight, pitch-dark in the blackout. I was snoozing soundly, cosily wrapped in the three pillows I had arranged into a pretend squishy dinghy (a routine I maintained until I was well into my teens). My repose couldn't have been more serene. Until I became aware of a slight movement near my ankle. My eyes popped open but it was so dark I could see nothing, so I reached down. It was as if the bed erupted! The air was rent by a screech more fearsome than a banshee, or a German doodlebug, and a jet-propelled bundle of white, almost luminous, fur hurtled into the air, landed on my face, and attempted to suffocate me while at the same time lacerating my cheeks with its claws. I have since met people – mostly women – who find such feline antics endearing. I didn't! Instead, I have been left with a cat phobia that has shown no sign of abating.

People often assume that I have got it in for cats because they eat birds. Of course they do and of course I don't approve, but that's not it. I just don't like them. I find them rather creepy. And why is that I wonder? Maybe something to do with that dark, dark night in Rochdale during the war, when I experienced shock and terror more heart-stopping than anything induced by any of the wild tigers, lions, leopards, elephants, or buffaloes that have featured on my television shows.

Mind you, talking of telly, those of you who remember *The Goodies* may recall perhaps the most repeated image we ever came up with: a rampant, giant of a creature, climbing the former Post Office Tower, now known as the BT Tower and terrifying London. That creature was called 'Kitten Kong' and it was … Yes, it was that fluffy, white cat! Maybe my early childhood was more inspiring than I thought!

# ANNE ATKINS

*Anne Atkins is a broadcaster, journalist and the author of three novels.*
*Anne was born in Bryanston, Dorset.*

I have so many and such happy pictures of my childhood home that my mind is a whirl! For instance, there was the day my father brought home a new wooden swing to hang from our pink horse-chestnut tree. I could climb the neighbour's fence and get a good rush on it. Then there was having tea on the lawn with my mother after school, while the lengthening shadows of the house crept up on us to tell us it was time to go in. I also remember the time that my brother explained to me that the dead squirrel I'd found in the garden wouldn't upset other squirrels, as animals aren't

*Anne and her mother.*

sentimental like that. I recall too, playing on my own in our spinney dwarfed by towering cow parsley. A blackbird hen darted late across the grass, singing sweetly before dusk. Yet, strangely, the one cameo which has decided to settle uppermost among the scattering leaves of my memories is a sad one.

It is the first time I recall my mother crying.

We had a balcony which faced south-west, cradling the late afternoon sun in its warmed red Victorian brick. Sometimes I enjoyed it alone; more often I sat there with my mother, perhaps asking her to untangle one of my string puppets or give me another of the maths puzzles she would invent.

On this occasion we were sitting just indoors, at the top of the stairs, near the balcony window. She was wearing that semi-glazed cotton frock I loved so well, with the geometrical patterns, over her familiar natural stockings and soft cross-over navy leather shoes.

She has just told me that my best friend, the one I collected all the trolls with, for which we made tiny clothes and furniture and played with for many a weekend afternoon, has just lost her father. He had shot himself. My mother is weeping for the family as she tells me this, and for my friend, of course, but mainly for the widow.

I can't understand this.

To lose a mother was a terrible thing: the worst I could imagine. Once I had dreamt that it had happened to me and woke distraught. When my mother asked the reason for my distress, in my foolish childishness I thought it would be rude to tell her of her imagined death and couldn't share my fears at first until she kindly coaxed it from me.

But to lose a husband? Why would that matter? Surely you could simply get another?

My mother was the greatest comfort I knew, for all my childhood and much of my adult life. Once I came home from school distressed by something or more likely, someone, and she set me on her knee and told me to dump it all on her.

'I am your dustbin,' she explained.

The years roll away and one wonders if one is even the same person.

She was eventually not: not at all; still happy, and loving, and full of gratitude for everything, yes. But she lost all her maths, suddenly, over two months one summer, some ten years ago or so. A few years later we gave my parents a home with us, after all their kindnesses. We showed them around their new home, the spacious bedroom we had allocated to them, their own bathroom, kitchen, and sitting room.

Then my mother wandered into the large family drawing room for which I had chosen the house, so like it was to the drawing room she had presided over in my childhood.

'Is this ours, too?' she asked, confused.

'It's all yours,' my husband said expansively. 'This is your home now.' How I loved him for it.

Alas, she only enjoyed it for a few weeks. Now I understand why my father still talks of missing his own mother, nearly half a century on. I will never get over her departure.

But my pain is nothing to what my father endures without her, even without her memory as she was for those last three years. Now, too, I understand what it is to love your life partner, and why my mother wept for my friend's mother all those years ago.

So because of this I now also understand that, great as my sorrow is to lose such an incomparable mother, my father's loss is far, far greater.

*Anne pictured with her two brothers, sister, and family dog.*

# Neil Sedaka

*Neil Sedaka was born in Brooklyn, USA. He is an award-winning singer-songwriter, musician and record producer.*

I remember growing up in a small, two-bedroomed apartment in Brighton Beach, Brooklyn, in the early 1940s. There were eleven of us: my sister, my mom, dad, granddad, grandma, five aunts and I. We had one bathroom. I was babied and pampered by all these women.

My grandmother was from Istanbul, Turkey. I remember she would play those wonderful 78 vinyl records sung in Ladino Spanish (old Spanish). I can still sing them today. We lived across from the Atlantic Ocean. I have great memories of swimming every day. It was a happy childhood. After World War Two, you could leave your doors unlocked; there were no drugs, burglaries, or terrorists. They are lovely memories and a part of my heart will always remain there. You can take Neil Sedaka out of Brooklyn, but you could never take the Brooklyn out of Neil Sedaka.

# MARGARET JAMES

*Margaret James is a novelist, journalist and editor. She is the author of numerous books, both fiction and non-fiction. Margaret was born in Hereford, England.*

My parents were both in the army. They met during the Second World War and got married in 1945. At this time, my mother was a penniless orphan who had no home of her own, and my father's widowed mother couldn't help them out financially. They lived in rented rooms for the first five years of their marriage, but somehow they managed to scrape together the deposit on a disused chapel in the suburbs of Hereford.

This converted chapel was my first childhood home. It had a tiny kitchen with a bath in one corner and there was a terrifying gas geyser over the bath. It terrified me, anyway, because it lit with a whoosh and a bang that made me think the whole house was going to fall down! There was no proper bathroom, but we had an outside lavatory in the tiny backyard. There was no garden, either, which must have been sad for my father, because he loved gardening.

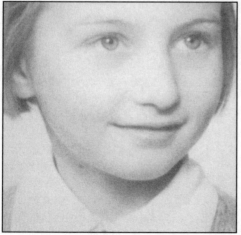

*Margaret, aged 5.*

We moved house again when I was six. Dad finally got his garden and he made full use of it: building a greenhouse (I always associate the smell of tomatoes in a greenhouse with Dad), cobbling together a very eccentric garden shed, tending a huge vegetable patch, planting a little orchard and growing some amazing lupins. I've never seen lupins like them since.

But, coming back to the former chapel – thanks to the scary geyser, I always had mixed feelings about bath night, and I'm still not very keen on baths, much preferring showers. When I was very small, my mother and I had baths together. But when it was my father's bath night – once a week in those days – the door to the kitchen was kept very firmly closed.

I had a tiny bedroom under the eaves of the roof. It was painted blue and I still have the blue cotton bedspread that was on my bed.

I've just looked up the little house. I see it is still there, and that the plaque which announces it was once a chapel is still on the façade. There is now a bay window where there was once a sash window, and of course there is double glazing. I hope the present owners have a bathroom, too!

# SIMON BATES

*Simon Bates was born in Birmingham, England. He is a DJ and radio presenter, best known for his Radio 1 show featuring the popular 'Our Tune' segment. He also regularly presented* Top of the Pops.

*Church Farm, Tong, Shifnal - Simon Bate's childhood home.*

Although it looks pretty grand and it may now have been thoroughly gentrified, it wasn't like that when my family lived there.

They were tenant farmers and the house was the best of British accidental design. It sort of grew organically over the centuries.

The fourteenth-century bit is on the left-hand side, with an old stone altar forming part of the wall of the cow barn, then there's the archway and the sixteenth- and seventeenth-century part, with a Victorian farmhouse completing the right-hand side.

For a long while it was one of the pubs in the village which explains the entrance way: good for horses and carts, I would think. And then, as the village lost its heart and the nearby castle was abandoned, there was no need for servants because there were no guests to be pampered. The pub closed, the clockmaker left and the church, where my family are buried, reverted to merely being a particularly beautiful village church, and a quiet one, where Dickens had Little Nell spend her last few hours on earth.

She was fictional; the churchwarden, who created a 'grave' for her and would con visitors out of pennies by relating Little Nell's story to gullible visitors in the latter part of the 1800s, was most definitely not.

My memories are less of the place and more of the animals.

My grandfather owned a pedigree herd of Guernsey cows that he doted on.

So, the memories are of my family, of course, but even more of the cattle.

The jokers: the blind cow that would make its way to its own stand perfectly happily, from wherever on the farm it happened to be.

The smell: the wonderful, sweet smell of cattle and hay ... of the grains the cows were fed from the local brewery, and the noise the cows made.

Of the way they would scuttle down the road and into the farm for summer afternoon milking and the special clatter of the aluminium buckets.

Oh, and the horses, too.

When we gave up the tenancy, I found, carefully wrapped in copies of *The Daily Express*, threadbare, almost useless tack from the days when we had Shire horses.

The village has changed inexorably; there's only one farmer left who I can say I know to have a pint with and so, really, now that my family are all dead, there's nothing left but shadows.

# ANNE NOLAN

*Anne Nolan is a member of the successful girl group, The Nolans, and has written an autobiography,* Anne's Song. *She was born in Dublin, Ireland.*

I have lived in nine different houses throughout my life, all with different memories, but I think the one that will always have a

*Anne, first from left, with her sisters.*

special place in my heart is the home I shared with my seven brothers and sisters and my mum and dad in Raheny, County Dublin, Ireland.

I have such fond memories of my early childhood there. I remember my mother tying rags on our shoes so that we could slide up and down on the lino in the hall after she had polished it. I clearly recall our first television; it was black and white obviously back in those times, though we had the first TV among all my friends. I'd sit looking at the test card for hours in awe.

Another lovely memory of that house is my sisters and I excitedly looking out of the window on Christmas Eve night, to see if we could see Santa Claus and his reindeers on their travels through the night sky. I would hold my breath, dying to see him but also scared of him spotting me!

I loved our little front garden in that house where we played all the usual games of that time, like skipping and chasing each other.

I am not sure if this house actually shaped my life, but it certainly taught me about the carefree wonderful joys of childhood, of companionship, of selflessness, and of love.

# ANNE BENNETT

*Anne Bennett was born in Birmingham, England. She is the best-selling author of nineteen books, specializing in sagas.*

I was born in a back-to-back house in the centre of Birmingham in 1949, the daughter of Irish immigrants. Our house at 301 Bell Barn Road opened onto the street, so we had a bigger cellar than those down the yard. We had a grating opening from the street where the coalman tipped the coal; in the cellar was a wide stone sink, all the junk that wouldn't fit in the minute house, and an aluminium bath on a hook behind the door.

Every Saturday night that bath was lifted down, and filled with kettles of water boiled on the gas stove in the little cubby hole at the top of the cellar steps that was called a kitchen, and my brother and I had a bath. Once washed, my dad would carry us upstairs wrapped in a towel. Our night clothes would be warming on the guard over the fire, our Mass clothes washed and ironed and hanging on the picture rail, and our shoes polished by Dad while we were in the bath.

Later, dressed for bed, warm and cosy, we sat before the roaring fire drinking cocoa and eating biscuits while Dad emptied the bath. He then played the chords of Irish jigs, reels, and songs from his native Ireland on his wind-up gramophone while Mum rubbed my hair dry. We always had our hair washed on Saturday for Mass the following morning.

We usually went to the pictures on Saturday morning, normally the Broadway we called the flea pit that cost thrupence. Any adult outside would know what we had been watching by the way we behaved as we erupted from the cinema later.

Apart from flashes, my earliest memory of those days was seeing the Coronation of Elizabeth II in 1953 when I had just turned four. A little while before my birthday, all the houses opening onto the street had had electricity fitted. So electric light in the cellar, the living room and our parents' bedroom replaced the gas, but sadly didn't extend to the attic where Shaun and I slept and we still made do with a candle. But we had electricity in the house and my mother went away to order a television on the Never-Never to watch the momentous coronation. Our television was an enormous box housing a tiny screen and it was inclined to go a bit snowy and crackly sometimes, which meant someone had to cavort around the room with the aerial. Thankfully it behaved beautifully on Coronation Day, which was just as well because all the residents from our yard, as well as relatives and friends, who had no electricity, were crammed into our house to watch it.

With the ceremony over, Coronation Day got better because we had a street party: sumptuous food and cake and sweets and as much pop as we wanted. And when we were quite finished there were games organised in the street and presents for every child, and I have still got my Coronation mug.

A child is very accepting of their home, but my mother must have found life quite hard at times. All the women had to do their washing in the brewhouse in the yard – taking turns at the boiler and then the maiding tub with the pummel and washboard, then the sink to starch the whites and then waiting to feed the whole lot through the mangle. They'd be praying for a dry day so the damp washing could be hung on the lines criss-crossing the yard and hoisted up on huge poles to flap dry in the sooty air. The yard also housed the miskins for the ashes, dustbins and lavatories at the bottom, shared by all of us.

And yet the community spirit was alive and well. Any woman would look after a child, fetch in shopping, fill coal scuttles and cook meals for the elderly or the infirm. They would help at childbirth, and care for the families if the mother was ill or had just given birth, and help lay out the dead at the end of their lives.

Bonfire night was a whole-street experience. The fire was built on the bombed buildings where streets and streets of houses, warehouses, shops, and factories had been flattened courtesy of the Luftwaffe. We would have been collecting burnable material for weeks and watched with excitement as the

*The road Anne lived in*

stack grew, but the Bell Barn Road boys had taken ownership of these bombed buildings and after making barricades and dens with the debris, they declared war on the kids from neighbouring Grant Street. We knew nothing would delight the Grant Street kids more than setting fire to the stack before Bonfire Night so our fathers took it in turns to guard it from about a fortnight beforehand. And on the night itself, money was pooled to buy fireworks and drinks for all. Some mothers would cook sausages, some baked potatoes, others made soup, yet another baked warm rolls and, if we were very lucky, some people would bring cinder toffee, or toffee apples. I remember those nights so well.

It was a time when you could leave your door open, but then no one had anything worth stealing and, though we were not rich, neither was anyone else. Our playground was the street and if we had no chalk for hopscotch half a house brick lobbed at the shell of a house at the end of the streets displaced a lump of plaster which worked just as well. We all had skipping ropes but even better was when the big girls would be inveigled into turning a big rope right across the street to play 'What's the time Mr Wolf?' – for there were no cars. Sometimes they would take a gang of us to the Calthorpe Park or Cannon Hill, and away we would go, with our jam sandwiches and our bottles of cold tea.

This time, this era has long gone, but I remember it all with great affection. We were given more freedom than a great many children today and I always thought it was a very happy place to live.

# SINEAD MORIARTY

*Sinead Moriarty was born and raised in Dublin, Ireland. She is a
journalist and the author of twelve novels. Sinead writes a weekly
column for the* Irish Independent *newspaper.*

When my grandmother passed away my grandfather became ill
and my mother, and the rest of us, moved in for a while to mind
him. We never moved out.

I was three years old at the time, and so I had the privilege of
growing up in a house with three parents: my mum and dad and
my granddad.

My sister and I shared the bedroom my mother had had as a
young girl. Our granddad was eccentric, funny, and very kind.
He shared his bedroom with my brother until, later on when my
brother was a teenager, we converted a small room downstairs so
he could have his own bedroom.

I have such vivid memories of going into my granddad to say
goodnight and getting into bed with him for a 'scorch'. Although
I realise this sounds like some kind of torture, it was in fact a
favourite nightly ritual. Having a 'scorch' with granddad meant
climbing into bed beside him and warming your toes on his hot-
water bottle.

This involved a fair amount of dexterity as his hot-water
bottle was one of those heavy porcelain ones that could burn
your toes if you left them on it too long. Once my feet were
warm, I'd kiss him goodnight and go back to my bed.

My granddad died at home when I was seventeen. We were
all there around his bed when he took his last breath. It was a
wonderful way to die – peacefully in his own bed, surrounded by
loved ones.

My mother still lives in the house she grew up in and every
time I call in I remember all the lovely memories of my youth.

The house feels like a huge part of our family's heritage and history. Two generations of children have grown up there and my own children now visit their granny and have sleepovers. Whereas I went for 'scorches' with porcelain hot-water bottles, my children get into bed with granny and have a 'scorch' with the electric blanket – probably far safer!

A house can be considered just bricks and mortar, but the house I grew up in is so much more. It's a house of precious memories and recollections of a happy childhood.

# Jo Wood

*Jo Wood is a model, television personality, author and entrepreneur. She is the former wife of the Rolling Stones guitarist Ronnie Wood and was born in Essex, England.*

I was nine years old when my father bundled us all into his Singer Gazelle estate car. We were going to see our new house or, rather, going to see our new house that was old. Up until then my home had been a brand new council house in Basildon. My father worked as an architectural model maker for Basildon council and had made the model of Basildon new town, so naturally we lived in one of the new houses. But now we (a family of five) were about to see our new house.

*Jo, as a young girl*

It wasn't a long journey from Basildon to Benfleet but it seemed to me that we had travelled miles. As we went up Vicarage Hill, Mum and Dad were so excited, I could feel that this house was different and it surely was. We drove down a tree-lined gravel driveway and, as we turned the corner, there stood a beautiful old house. It was like something out of a fairy story. The house was huge, especially to me as I was so small. Its pointed roofs, its big chimneys built of stone and its leaded windows took my breath away.

'This house is over three hundred years old,' said my father. 'And they say there is a vicar buried under the front doorstep!'

It was an old vicarage and it was beautiful. The current vicar had moved into a new-build opposite and the church had sold the land next door. My dad was given the job of designing the development and while looking at the plans had noticed this old vicarage. He ended up buying it for £5,000.

Over the next few years, my parents renovated and turned the vicarage into a loving home. This house gave me a love of historic houses, ignited my passion for interior design and furnished my dreams of the future. We had chickens and a vegetable garden and a huge, huge oak tree that I would climb without fear to the very top with the boy from next door. My brothers and I built camps in the garden and would camp out all night. We dug the garden (well, Mum and Dad did, I just helped) and found an old well which I thought was magical. We spent the summers building a sort of treehouse. My sister was born there. That house opened my eyes to all possibilities … It was a wonderful start to my life.

*The Old Vicarage, Benfleet.*

# NERYS HUGHES

*Nerys Hughes is an actress famed as Sandra in* The Liver Birds. *She won the Variety Club Television Actress of the Year Award for her work in* The District Nurse, *a series that was written for her. Nerys was born in Rhyl, Flintshire, Wales.*

I was born and brought up in a seaside town in North Wales. In the summer people streamed in on trains, charabancs, and cars for their holidays, day trips, and Sunday school trips. The town was a jaunty holiday mecca with shops and booths selling buckets and spades, ice creams, fish and chips, naughty postcards and kiss-me-quick hats. It was the happiest, noisiest, most carefree holiday place, which people visited for two weeks of the year for their annual holidays – *and I lived there!*

Our house was on a road which led up to the beach. In the morning, I would wake to the sound of clip-clop, clip-clop as Mr Jones took his donkeys to the sands for donkey rides. Next would be the holiday makers, trailing their spades (metal in those days) along the pavement. My sister and I would get dressed for a quick breakfast then run up the road to the beach. Life was so safe in those days. We stayed on the beach, built sandcastles, collected shells, and paddled in the sea, then ran home for our dinner, shaking off the sand in the outside washhouse before going into the house. The back door was always unlocked.

My father (who was the most fun dad anyone could have) had an ironmonger's shop in the town. He used to come home for his dinner (we called our midday meal 'dinner' and the evening meal 'supper') and, when he went back to work, sometimes our mother would take us along the prom to the other end of the town. There were gardens there, a huge swimming pool and paddling pool, an outdoor amphitheatre for entertainments and 'Punch and Judy';

there was also a roller skating rink. There was a big pavilion where comedians and singers came to give variety shows in the evening, and there were sun shelters and seats all along the way. It had everything – *and I lived there*!

Every evening before supper, our dad would take us for a walk to feed the seagulls. They caught the bread we threw on the wing and entered the spirit of things in a way that seagulls these days seem to have lost. They are so predatory and frightening now, aren't they?

The centre of our lives was the chapel. My father was the organist and we attended each Sunday service and Sunday school in the afternoon. But it was never repressive, just the social and moral hub of our lives.

But the most exciting place our father took us to, at least once a week, was the fairground. We were allowed two rides and an ice cream. Swooping 'Figure of Eight' rides from immense heights, 'Bucket Seat' rides that swung you round, and dodgems that jarred your spine, and a ride which stuck you to the side of a drum as the floor fell away. Terrifying. My dad loved it all and so did we!

Some evenings we would go for a ride into the country. We had a Rover 10 car that had a heavy body and small engine and sometimes we all had to get out to go up hills. We had many relations who lived on farms, so often we would be invited to have bacon and fresh eggs for supper – or we might stop at Percy Parry's and have the best fish and chips ever, eaten with our fingers from newspaper on the way home in the car.

*Nerys as a young girl.*

My life as a child in the summer in that town was a magical mix of sea, sun and fresh air and '*ysbryd* holidays' – the spirit of holidays – *and I lived there*!

# RUTH BADGER

*Ruth Badger was born in Wolverhampton, England. She is a businesswoman, a television presenter and was runner-up in the second series of BBC's* The Apprentice.

I had a really happy childhood and a big influence on it was that I lived in the same house from birth until I got married at twenty-four and left home. My grandparents lived ten doors away which made me feel like we owned the street as I was always playing between the houses.

Our home was a terraced house which looked small from the front but was like the TARDIS when you stepped inside. We had a huge garden and as I was a tomboy this was heaven to me!

The garden was my playground where I could use my vivid imagination. At the front of the garden was the seating area; in the middle was the grass area where I played games with my brother. My dad watched me from his greenhouse, and my mum always kept her eye on me, as I was always in trouble or falling out of trees. The best part of the garden was at the very back as I was banned from going there! Here I would build dens, climb trees, and jump out to scare my brother. Looking back, it's no wonder my parents didn't like me playing at the back of the garden, as I would often dig underground to build tunnels and dens. I had no idea how dangerous that was. I would go home and be filthy but God I had fun!

My brother now owns that house, which is nice as I can still go home, and it's lovely to know happy memories are still being made there.

*Ruth, with her older brother, in their back garden.*

# GORDON HASKELL

*Gordon Haskell is a musician, songwriter, vocalist and music producer. He is a former member of the band King Crimson and had massive success as a solo artist with the album* Harry's Bar *from which his single, 'How Wonderful You Are' became the most requested song ever on Radio 2.*

I have had what I can only describe as an unusual life. I still have an immense admiration for my mother who raised me, along with my brother and sister, on her own in a council house in Dorset. She, as a war widow, had to wait years to be housed, queueing up for months on end. She was treated abominably by those who robbed so many of their husbands at such a young age. I learned at a very young age of the class war.

The house that made me really came many, many years later when I moved to an island in the Aegean Sea, Greece.

I had to wait until I was sixty-one years old before I felt I had found my home. There are many reasons for this strange fact. The first is that my father was of Greek origin, and I had always felt awkward and uncomfortable trying to fit in with my English family. My brother and sister had a different father and my mother had been raised in a tradition I felt no affinity with. It was not her fault. It was mostly to do with the consequences of world wars, and the British colonial way of thinking that she had been indoctrinated with and had swallowed hook line and sinker.

The home and environment now, in 2016, are perfect in every way.

As a child, I remember craving the sort of food one only finds naturally growing here, so I now have the healthy food I need. And all the aches, pains, and arthritis I used to suffer from have disappeared. The people here are without any sense of snobbery and greet me with warmth and kindness, something I yearned for so much in my childhood. The house is very humble with just one bedroom built into the roof and is ample for my needs; it is simple in design. I have a wonderful view of the sea, a harbour, and mountains, with another island in the distance. The sunrises and sunsets are beautiful and, with all this beauty, I am filled with wonder at how magnificent the world can be if we look for it. For with beauty, love, a good diet, and a simple shelter there is no need to be rich. Greed is non-existent here. This place is all I ever dreamed of and compared to the struggle of making a living and finding a home in England, it seems so in reach for the humblest of men. I have had seven full years of complete happiness. I am sixty-nine years old and most of my life has been spent arguing with people in England who said what I was dreaming of didn't exist.

I am glad I lived long enough to prove them all completely and utterly wrong.

The house I live in now is the house that made me. I am happy at last. I have come home. I am finally at peace.

*The view from Gordon's home in Greece.*

# NIGEL HAVERS

*Born in London, Nigel Havers is an actor. He has appeared in stage, film and television roles including as Lord Andrew Lindsay in the film* Chariots of Fire *for which he earned a BAFTA nomination. On television, he is best known as rascal Lewis Archer in* Coronation Street *and as Dr Tom Latimer in the comedy* Don't Wait Up.

In the mid-fifties, Dad bought a tumbledown cottage in Suffolk for the princely sum of two hundred pounds. With no electricity or running water and no facilities beyond an old tin bath, I expect Mum thought it less of a bargain than it now seems. It was a wild and woolly place; it still is, a world away from the fleshpots of Newmarket, eight miles to the west.

The cottage gradually took shape. Mum was in charge of the interior and Dad became obsessed with the garden. He wasn't keen on flowers but set out on a quest to fill the place with every variety of British tree and vegetable. Every so often, a few bulbs and cuttings were smuggled into place by Mum, who longed for a bit of colour, but these anarchic uprisings were soon spotted and dealt with – apart from the roses, which were tended with loving care.

Harry Carr, the Queen's jockey, lived in the next village over and one year he was riding Parthia in the Derby, my brother Phil and I decided to have a pocket-money flutter – so did Dad, whose pocket money was obviously rather more generous than ours. Suffice to say we had a holiday in Italy that year – go on, my son!

I went to a local prep school called Nowton Court. It was a wonderfully romantic mock-gothic building set in glorious parkland, run by a rather eccentric family who were extremely keen on the arts – the rest is history.

So there we have it – my life has sprung fully formed from those few paragraphs: my career, my life-long love of racing, gardens and the glorious Suffolk countryside. One day, when I've earned enough money, maybe when I'm about ninety, I shall buy a Seago painting and spend the rest of my days gazing at those fabulous skies and remembering my carefree Suffolk youth.

# JANE FALLON

*Jane Fallon was born in Harrow, London. She is a novelist and former television producer. Her long-term partner is Ricky Gervais.*

We moved into the flat above my parents' shop when I was two. My mum and dad, five children and the dog, and the cat who arrived soon after. As I got older I needed to find more and more unlikely places where I could get some peace and quiet and indulge my passion for reading: on top of the water tank in the attic; crammed inside the dog's kennel in the back garden, with the scratchy straw and our fat Labrador Tim breathing Winalot breath on me; perched on a high, smelly, compost heap that reeked so much no one else would go near it. I needed guaranteed alone time. There were only so many hours in the day and I wanted to spend as many of them as I could with my nose in a book.

Living above a shop that sold sweets was a challenge for a small child. We kids were on strict chocolate rations in order to prevent us from consuming all the profits – we were allowed to choose one bar each on a Sunday afternoon. But when I was about eight it occurred to me that I could just wander downstairs in the middle of the night and help myself. Shortly afterwards my mum found my stash melting under my pillow (I was no criminal mastermind) and a lock appeared on the door from the flat to the shop.

We moved into a house when I was a teenager and I remember thinking how weird it was that people could just walk past your windows and see in. I never got used to it.

*The shop above which Jane lived as a child.*

# FENELLA FIELDING

*Fenella Fielding is an actress, famed for her distinctive husky voice and for her roles in two of the* Carry On *movies. She was born in London.*

When I was young, we lived in Clapton, in the borough of Hackney, in a small mansion flat. We had three bedrooms – one for my parents, one for my brother, and one for me plus a sort-of nanny person. Nearby was the Venus Pencil factory with an enormous Venus pencil on its frontage. I was very proprietorial about this. I took it for granted that the factory was full of pencils in the same way that the immense Christmas cracker dragged on by clowns in a pantomime finale was full of

*Jane revisits her childhood home at Rowhill Mansions*
*(© Simon McKay)*

normal-sized crackers which they threw into the audience at the end of the show.

My brother, Bas, was three or four years older than me, so he came home from school a bit later than I did, which gave me a chance to invade his bedroom. I had been signed up to a worthy but boring read called *The Children's Newspaper*, but Bas had those exciting boys' magazines: the *Hotspur* and the *Champion*, and I could read them fast before he got home, wallowing in the glamour of 'Dixie' Dale, the popular sportsmaster, and the real horridness of Mr Smugg, a most unpleasant teacher, forever doling out lines and punishing everyone in sight.

Bas didn't like anyone else to read his magazines before he had, and he used to try to stop me doing so by hiding them. I remember one time when I invaded his bedroom; I looked and looked. I went under the bed. Nothing. I climbed up and looked in the wardrobe. Nothing. Suddenly, I had an inspiration. My old rocking horse was there. I pulled out the rocking horse's tail, and there was the *Hotspur* rolled up with the *Champion*. He'd made an almost successful attempt to hide them from me, but I won!

# JILL MANSELL

*Jill Mansell is an author who has written twenty-seven novels to date.
She grew up in the Cotswolds and now lives in Bristol.*

I grew up in the Cotswolds, in a village a mile from Badminton
where the international horse trials are held. Our tiny village
school was very *Cider with Rosie*. Our house was built of
Cotswold stone and the walls were very thick, which meant all
the windows had window-seats. These were my favourite places
to sit, with red velvet curtains you could hide behind.

We lived opposite a farm, and twice a day the cows would be
brought along the main road for milking. On the other side of our
house was the village church, so we always had a good view of
weddings. The tradition of village children tying shut the church
gates until the wedding guests gave them money meant people
used to climb through a well-worn gap in the yew hedge and
escape through our garden instead. I recently went back to attend
a friend's funeral and saw that the hedge is now beautifully
manicured and ten-feet high but the broken-down section is still
clearly visible at ground level.

In the garden my favourite tree to climb was the holly tree,
which is less uncomfortable than it sounds, because the leaves
were only on the outer branches. It was a fantastic tree to hide in.
I also spent endless hours hitting a tennis ball up against the
garage wall because my mum desperately wanted me to be good
at tennis … but sadly that never happened. The other enduring
memories of growing up in our house are the iced-up windows in
winter, the water freezing in the taps, and needing to wear
several vests and jumpers at a time. Oh, and the endless power
cuts, of course!

It's been so lovely, remembering these details. As a teenager I
longed for the bustle and bright lights of a city lifestyle and

couldn't wait to leave my rural childhood behind. But all these years later I'd really love to move back. Who knows, maybe I will!

# Jeffrey Holland

*Jeffrey Holland is a stage and screen actor. He is best known for his role as Spike in the classic comedy series* Hi-de-Hi!

The first home I remember was a little two-bedroomed mid-terrace house in the industrial West Midlands town of Walsall. I lived there from 1947 until 1966 when I was twenty-one.

My father had been demobbed after the war and we were given a prefab when I was born a year later. We stayed there for just a year.

Then we all moved to the little terraced house after one of the coldest winters in history. It had an old brick-built water heater, called a 'copper', in the back kitchen which was heated from underneath by a coal fire. There was no bathroom and the toilet was down the backyard next to the coalhouse. Our weekly bath was taken on a Friday night in an old galvanised tin bath, which hung on the wall next to the kitchen. I would be first and then be packed off to bed so that my parents could then take theirs. The hot water came from an electric boiler that my mum did her washing with, and I remember that the tap just about reached over the top of the tin bath on the kitchen floor!

It was a simple life and then suddenly there was excitement when it was announced that a baby was on the way! I was three years old at the time and had no idea where babies came from. All I knew was that my mother was going to have a baby. In those days, babies were usually born at home, so all I was aware of was that our family doctor's visits became more and more frequent with the passing weeks. I was curious, but of course was told nothing, until one day when the doctor came to visit my mother I could bear it no more! I suddenly knew where babies came from!

As the doctor went up the stairs clutching his black leather

medical case, I turned proudly to my anxious father and said,
'The baby's in the bag, isn't it, Dad?'
Happy days!

# SUE MOORCROFT

*Sue Moorcroft is an author, columnist and journalist.*

As an Army kid, I don't remember my first three homes and have scant memories of the fourth. The first home that I have clear and vivid memories of is a top-floor flat overlooking Ta' Xbiex yacht marina in Malta.

As the block of flats was (and still is) triangular and our flat was situated on the front corner, the flat was triangular, too, with balconies that wrapped around it. From those balconies I could sometimes see one of my brothers fishing or the other on his paper round; I could watch for Dad's car as he came home from work at GHQ in the Auberge de Castille in Valletta; Mum nipping out to the local shop; and, when I was home with chicken pox, I could watch the other children waiting for the school bus in the road below.

My favourite view was across the road, over Gzira Gardens and the marina, to Manoel Island. The marinas on both sides of Sliema creek bobbed with boats: anything from inflatables, to sailing yachts, to large motor boats. Little did I know as I sat in the sun and watched the comings and goings of the boat owners, that I would one day use the setting for a novel, *The Wedding Proposal.*

The block of flats has been renamed and buildings have grown up around it but, when I lived there, there was a play park at the rear of the flats and a fair amount of land that seemed to have little purpose but to allow us freedom. We built dens, collected grasshoppers and caterpillars, rolled around in an old oil drum, played games such as 'Billy Kick the Can', and spent a lot of time pretending to be Superman. We also played in Gzira Gardens or fished between the boats of the marina. My family hasn't yet forgotten that I once fell in the water and someone wrote to the *Times of Malta* about it and the British Army kids who didn't know how to behave. Maybe they thought I was in danger, but I'd gained my bronze personal survival swimming medal before I was six.

My happiest childhood memories are all of Malta.

# BEL MOONEY

*Bel Mooney is an author, a journalist, columnist, and broadcaster, and writes a weekly column for the* Daily Mail. *She was born in Liverpool.*

My parents moved to a new Liverpool Corporation estate called The Green when I was about six. They had read in the *Liverpool Echo* that the nearby primary school in Wavertree, Northway, had an excellent record for getting pupils through the Eleven-Plus. Mum and Dad cared so much about education they put in for a council house transfer from West Derby, which meant a massive rent increase, since the brand new flats were sought after. So we moved into the clean, smart low-rise four-bedroom flat – and Dad worked overtime to pay for it. This was definitely a step up in the world.

24b was on the top (second) floor, overlooking Queen's Drive. So my sleep was punctuated by the sound of the number 81 bus changing gear, and illuminated by permanent light from the dual carriageway, shining through thin cotton curtains. During the long snowy winters, the windows froze in starburst patterns on the inside and my brother and I dashed across icy lino to dress in the kitchen by the electric fire.

The flat had two balconies and the back one was where Mum hung the washing. There was also a 'chute' which the rubbish went down. In the wall at the end of the balcony was a heavy steel handle on a plate that opened down and outwards to reveal a rather smelly black hole into which the rubbish was thrown. You would hear tin cans clattering down past the middle floor (which shared the chute, of course) to the ground, where all the rubbish festered for a week until the bin men came to collect it. These tough Liverpool workers, like the coal men, always seemed to have a ready grin splitting the accumulated grime.

My favourite toys were not dolls but teddy bears, and each

night I went to bed with three. One day my parents bought me a new hot-water bottle in the shape of a teddy bear. He was blue rubber, with big eyes, a curving smile and round ears; the hot-water bottle stopper was embedded in his head. I loved Hot Teddy, who joined his plush cousins in my bed as an essential companion during those cold nights in the 1950s, when snow drifted three-feet deep around the flats.

*Bel Mooney as a child.*

But the years pass and rubber perishes and one day – horror – Hot Teddy sprang a leak. 'He can't go to bed with you anymore' said Mum. I agreed of course (what child wants water in the bed?) but assumed Hot Teddy would be allowed to live. Sadly, my father saw no reason to keep a useless hot-water bottle and threw Hot Teddy away. Down the chute he went, to lie in the darkness at the bottom as cans and peelings gradually buried him. Of course, I didn't know this until after the event. I was horrified, but this feeling turned to rage and grief when my poor father tried to turn the whole thing into a joke. He was such a kind man; how could he realise how cruel he was being to say, 'I heard him calling goodbye and crying your name, all the way down to the bottom of the chute'?

That was it. I sobbed in my bedroom and wouldn't come out.

126

My poor parents were horrified; how could they know that their over-imaginative little girl imbued everything with real life? That is why, as an adult, I had no problem in agreeing that my own daughter's doll, Primrose, was real. Of course she was! This is the message of Margery Williams's classic *The Velveteen Rabbit* and of the wonderful *Toy Story* trilogy – all our precious toys become real if they are loved enough.

About once a year we visit Liverpool, where I still have family. As the M62 becomes an ordinary road at the Rocket shopping area (where we used to buy our food and fish and chips on a Friday) I feel I'm coming home. The now-enlarged council estate is in front on the right, and I still like that simple brick-built 1950s architecture. Now I often wonder if the flats are still served by a chute for their rubbish, but somehow I doubt it. Now, surely, they will have recycling bins. Gladly I imagine the black holes of multiple rubbish chutes safely sealed, sparing anymore broken toys or Hot Teddies that sad, long fall into darkness.

# TRISHA ASHLEY

*Trisha Ashley is an author. Her romantic comedy* Every Woman for Herself *was nominated by readers as one of the top three romantic novels of the last fifty years. Trisha originates from St Helens in west Lancashire.*

My parents married in the difficult post-war years and my father, who had been apprenticed to a tailor before being called up, eventually found shift work in a clothing factory. Meanwhile Mum, with no capital or retail experience, bravely started up a shoe shop in vacant premises on the outskirts of St Helens in Lancashire, two doors down from my grandmother's haberdashery business. I was born there, in the bedroom above the shop, the second of two children.

Mum and Dad, both intelligent and creative people, were not afraid of hard work and started up various small enterprises to make ends meet: often working late into the night producing costume jewellery, Christmas crackers and glittery Christmas cards, among other things. They also had a small hand-printing press, the rhythmic thump of which was the lullaby that used to send me to sleep.

Behind the shop, shut off by a sliding wooden door, lay a living room and a quarry-tiled kitchen, with a separate washroom. When the stockroom eventually expanded, my father knocked the washhouse through into the kitchen to make extra living space. In spring, the yard smelled of the night-scented stocks, nasturtiums and snapdragons that my mother sowed in the borders and one of my earliest memories is toddling down the brick path and burying my shoes at the furthest end, using my small red metal spade. I still prefer to walk about in my bare feet...

All the inspiration for my Lancashire novels is rooted here: my paternal grandfather could slip in and out of dialect at will and was a wealth of stories, legends, monologues and songs while Dad was – and still is – keenly interested in local history. The shoe shop directly inspired that in *Chocolate Shoes and Wedding Blues*; while my grandmother's haberdashery, when years later we finally came to clear it, was the prototype of Miss Honey's in *Wish Upon a Star*.

When I was small, St Helens was still very much an industrial town, with Pilkington's glass factory at its heart, bordered by row upon row of terraced houses. But on Sundays we would walk out into the country, or to a nearby beautiful park with a boating lake and, in season, stunning displays of rhododendrons and bluebell woods.

*Trisha as a young girl.*

Further excursions, before we could afford a car, were made by bus to Southport or across the Mersey on the ferry to New Brighton.

It's all there, a rich soup of memories to dip into when I'm writing – and I still adore the smell of new leather!

130

# ALAN TITCHMARSH MBE DL

*Alan Titchmarsh is a broadcaster, gardener and novelist. He is best known for presenting* Gardener's World *and* The Alan Titchmarsh Show. *Alan was appointed a Member of the Order of the British Empire for services to horticulture and broadcasting and also made Deputy Lieutenant of the County of Hampshire.*

I lived there between the ages of one and fifteen years. It was a soot-blackened stone-built terrace house in Ilkley – a Yorkshire town famed for its heather- and bracken-covered moorland and the song: 'On Ilkla Moor, baht 'at', which is really all anyone knows about it – except that now it boasts a Betty's Café where you can enjoy wonderful Yorkshire rarebit. The town nestles in a valley below the moor, on either side of the River Wharfe. Wharfedale is *my* dale, and the house in Nelson Road is still there, smaller than I remember it, which should, I suppose, come as no surprise. We were within walking distance of a 'top shop' and a 'bottom shop' – both of them off-licences selling confectionery and pop and a few groceries, and at the bottom of the street was Samuel Ledgard's bus garage, against whose brick wall we would play football in winter and cricket in summer. (I had my first Woodbine in the bushes behind it and managed to avoid my mum finding out by sucking half a dozen Polo mints in rapid succession.)

The house was next but one to the top end of the terrace. Downstairs, when I was a nipper, you'd have found a kitchen at the back and a sitting room at the front, a door from which led to the coal cellar. There were two bedrooms and a loo on the first floor, and my bedroom and a bathroom on the top floor in what was the attic until my dad, a plumber and an adept do-it-yourselfer, converted it and later put in central heating. We must have been the first folk in the street to boast full CH – but then the radiators came from someone else's house; someone who was having an upgrade. It didn't matter – we were warm at last, even if we did have to 'bleed' the radiators of air every night before bed.

My dormer window had a great view of the moors in one direction and the village of Middleton in the other, and with my window open I could hear the town hall clock strike the hours. It was thanks to my dad that I have so many memories of the house in which I grew up, for it was he who built a desk and bookcases in my bedroom and who, in the weeks before Christmas, would disappear into the cellar which became out of bounds to my sister and I. The sound of sawing and the smell of paint should have given us a clue as to what was going on, especially when on Christmas morning I would discover that Santa had left me a smartly painted zoo, or a garage, or a fort. I cannot think of it now without a tear coming to my eye.

On the rug in front of the fire, Mum would pin tissue-paper patterns to fabric bought at the Remnant Shop, and create – with her Singer sewing machine – the most magical dresses for dances and fire-station socials (my dad was a part-time fireman). I can remember them leaving by the front door in the evening, Mum having asked us, 'Will I do?' I still recall the pride I felt at her beauty and elegance. No other mum looked a patch on her.

The front garden was no more than a square of lawn, surrounded by a dusty border where lily of the valley sprang up, and bounded by a privet hedge, but it was in the back garden, just across the back lane, where I learnt that I could grow things – sowing seeds in pots and trays in a little polythene greenhouse that I built myself from lumps of timber Dad brought home from work, and polythene sheeting from the local hardware shop. The smell of newly unrolled polythene can transport me back more than fifty years in an instant.

We left the house when I was sixteen – to move to a pebble-dashed semi up the smarter end of town. But a part of my heart still resides in Nelson Road in a little house and garden that constituted a magical and secure beginning for a small boy who liked growing things.

# DON WARRINGTON MBE

*Don Warrington is a Trinidadian-born British actor. He is a stage, film and television star, best known for his role as Philip Smith in the classic sitcom* Rising Damp. *He was appointed Member of the Order of the British Empire in 2008.*

I had several childhood homes. The one I remember clearest was my grandmother's house. I suspect that's because I was at my happiest there.

My mother had gone to England, and had left us, my brother and I, in Trinidad with a woman, although not a relative, we were told to address as Aunty Lucy. She resented having to look after us, and so my grandmother took us to live with her and our sister. My grandmother's home was welcoming and warm with room to roam. She kept chickens, pigs, and goats on a patch of land on the opposite side of the road. I enjoyed feeding them and getting to know them. Sometimes I would watch my grandmother slaughter the chickens. We would then eat them. At the back of her house she grew fruit trees – tropical fruit trees, big enough and exciting enough for a small boy to get lost in and indulge his imagination.

Things changed when my mother took my brother and I to England.

# RICK GUARD

*Rick Guard originates from Chorley, Lancashire. He is a contemporary jazz singer and songwriter. Rick is a supporter of the Alzheimer's Society, contributing the proceeds of his album to the charity.*

Even writing the name 'Greycot' gives me a feeling of warmth and pride. It was the family home, the place where I spent all my life until age twenty-two, my comfort blanket, my adventure playground, my primary universe of memories.

As an adult now, with a wife and a six-year-old boy of my own, I am acutely aware of how lucky I was to live in our imposing, detached, quirky 1920s house in Lancashire, surrounded by immaculate gardens and a fruit orchard. The experience has seen me strive to provide the same environment for my boy. We now live in a very green and friendly area in line with those memories.

I still go well out of my way to drive past the old house whenever I'm in the area. On sight, the wonderful memories of my three siblings and our busy parents maintaining the household come flooding back. Writing this, it strikes me that you experience the entirety of life in the microcosm of a house: fun, fear, happiness, death, disappointment, pleasure, comfort, peace, safety, love, the list is endless.

I will always remember that, when my mother was very confused with her Alzheimer's, she would find great solace in the concept of 'home', even if it was a blurred memory of a fireplace from one house and a garden from another; there was pure comfort in the notion of its existence.

For me, the enduring memory of my family home 'Greycot' is that it was a never-ending resource of boundless adventure; every tree, every nook and cranny gave new potential for my imagination to be sparked.

I've made it my goal to provide such a playground of memories for my offspring. Thank you Greycot: it's someone else's playground of memories now.

# Sandra Chapman

*Sandra Chapman is a journalist and editor, writing a popular weekly column for the Belfast newspaper, the* News Letter. *She was born in Northern Ireland.*

My parents moved home four times as the family got bigger. I was born in the first house – a typical Irish-style cottage with a thatched roof which one day went up in flames, a common enough occurrence then in rural Ulster.

*Shanemullagh House*

My mother hated the second house, and the third. She loved her final home, though by the time she lived there most of her children had left and she had it mostly to herself. For us children, though, the third house was a dream place. Shanemullagh House, County Londonderry , was a small manor house of Georgian vintage, with loads of rooms, huge grounds, a tennis court, orchard, courtyard, and wooded walks ideal for hiding out with boyfriends or girlfriends.

The first Christmas in this house saw us almost completely cut off from the outside world, with huge snow drifts filling the winding driveway. My mother resorted to buying gas heaters to keep the place warm for Christmas as its ancient central heating refused to work. I resolved to make the place look magical that

Christmas for the younger members of the family. We had a big tree full of lights framed in the French windows of the drawing room, with bunches of holly everywhere, including on top of the pictures which hung on the walls, and homemade decorations all around. By the time Mum and I had finished it was like something out of a Christmas card.

The snow had begun to fall early that Christmas Eve. By the time I had got home from work by bus and trudged up the driveway, I arrived at the massive front door looking like the proverbial snowman. The smallest children were in a state of heightened excitement, as they were convinced Santa would have no trouble landing his sleigh on the tennis court! My bedroom was a large room at the front of the house with bathroom attached. From the bathroom I could open French doors out to a balcony. That night, before I got into bed, I decided to step out on to the balcony as the snow had finally stopped falling. I found myself gazing out on a deep cobalt blue sky with twinkling stars and a moon shining down on unbroken snow. It was a truly magical sight, and I would not have been at all surprised if Santa and his sleigh had appeared in an ark across the sky in front of me. The children never did find out if he landed on the tennis court as it was covered in snow. Thankfully!

# ED BALLS

*Ed Balls is a former cabinet minister, born in Norwich, Norfolk. He is a Senior Fellow at Harvard University Kennedy School's Mossavar-Rahmani Center for Business and Government and a visiting Professor to the Policy Institute at King's College, London. He was appointed Chairman of Norwich City F.C. in 2015.*

Our first family home was in the small village of Bawburgh, just outside Norwich. A three-bedroomed detached house, it looked out at the back across a huge water meadow to the village bridge and a water mill which churned the River Yare as it flowed by.

In the winter, the meadow often flooded, with water rising up over our back garden. But we always had a great view. Because this was no ordinary house. And in our village, everyone knew where we lived – our house was the 'upside-down house'.

Upside-down. Topsy-turvy. The wrong way round. And every day we knew it.

Our first family car was a Mini. When my Dad drove us up Church Lane and then into the drive of our house, we would clamber out and run to the front door. But then we would go up the stairs to the living room and kitchen. Yes, up. Or down the stairs to the bedrooms.

My bedroom was at the back of the house, which I shared with my younger brother after he was born. Right outside my window, just a few feet down was the back garden. Once when the health visitor was coming to visit, my mum says she took her down to see a supposedly sleeping me. But I had opened the window and jumped out and was playing football in the garden.

Bedrooms on the ground floor were a bonus, of course. The real reason the house was upside-down was to get great views from the upstairs rooms. To the back, we could stare over the water meadow and watch the birds and sometimes a boat go by;

to the front, I remember sitting with my mum and watching the rubbish lorry tipping itself up, as the bin-men waved to me at the upstairs window.

We still had a back kitchen door. But it opened out onto a big wooden balcony, which you could reach by climbing up a wooden staircase to the side of the house. In the summer, we could sit outside and have our breakfast and admire the view. In the winter you could stand up there and throw snowballs down on visitors in the garden below.

Our garden had a big patch of grass, broken up by two big trees but with plenty of space to play football. Norwich v Ipswich, usually. Norwich always won.

Beyond the grass was a big vegetable patch, bordered at the bottom by a stream which ran round the meadow to the river. It was a good place to fish with nets.

Next door they had a pond full of carp like big goldfish. In the early mornings, a heron used to

*Ed, in his garden, aged five.*

come and sit by the pond to do some fishing.

It was a really nice house, with one small drawback. There was no proper mains drainage. Instead, we had a septic tank in the garden for sewerage which we shared with our neighbours with the pond. And when the big truck came to empty the tank, it really, really stank. Even up on our balcony.

# MICHELLE GAYLE

*Michelle Gayle is a recording artist, songwriter, actress and author and has been nominated for two Brit Awards. She is well-known for her role in* Eastenders *as Hattie Tavernier.*

When I think of my childhood home, two things instantly come to mind: music and food!

Being brought up by my West Indian parents meant that they tapped into memories of 'back home'. When they weren't playing albums by reggae legends such as John Holt or Bob Marley (my dad is Jamaican), or calypso classics like 'Feeling Hot, Hot, Hot' (my mum, Grenadian), they were tuned into specialist shows on Radio London – a station that seemed to embrace London's west Indian contingent.

Music woke us up via our radio alarm clock; it provided the atmosphere for joyful party moments, pathos for sad ones. And music was always there, playing in the background, while my mum or dad got on with what otherwise might have been tedious cooking.

Thursday was pronounced Dad's cooking night and it was (secretly) my favourite – sorry Mum. Always the same meal: curried pork chops with dumplings and plantain (a savoury banana). We'd sing along – usually to Gladys Knight – as I helped Dad chop the onions. (I think Gladys was the bit my dad loved best.) Then I'd lay the table as he allowed time for the meat to soften. When dinner was served, I think it was my sister's favourite meal too, judging from the glee on her face whenever it arrived.

Years later, when I was doing a photo shoot in LA, I mentioned my dad's love of Gladys Knight. The photographer happened to be great friends with her and was, in fact, doing a photo shoot with her the next day. She invited me along and I took a photograph with Gladys that I gleefully dropped on my dad's lap once I returned.

'Oh Gladys,' he sighed.

# Sanjeev Bhaskar OBE

*Sanjeev Bhaskar was born in Ealing, London. He is an actor, comedian, author, and broadcaster, best known for his work in* Goodness Gracious Me *and* The Kumars at No. 42. *He received an Officer of the Order of the British Empire in 2005 and was given the Outstanding Achievement in Television Award in 2015 at the Asian Awards. He is married to Meera Syal.*

I guess my formative years were spent in a maisonette above a launderette in Heston, Middlesex. With no double glazing or central heating, and just two small gas heaters for the whole place, my parents, sister and I retreated to the living room for the entire winter season. Like bears. We ate, slept, played and watched TV in that room. Apart from the interpersonal warmth, this room was above the boilers of the launderette and hence kept warm with a pleasant constancy. A necessary journey to the loo or bathroom required a mini Arctic expedition, with layers of wrapping, forward thinking regarding unfastening clothes, and even having a hot-water bottle on standby. The immersion heater meant that hot water for baths had to be planned in advance. Many a time I ran a bath only for the hot water to peter out at ankle depth. My father improvised rudimentary double glazing in the bathroom, consisting of a thick, clear plastic sheet, nailed to the window frame. All this seemed to do in reality was to trap and freeze the moisture between window and plastic, so neither could you see out nor could you let air in.

Spring would mark the exodus of the family back to our bedrooms. Although I was always happy to get back to my books and posters of Monty Python, The Beatles, Elvis and Roger Moore, within a few days I longed for the 'camping' style joint adventure of the one room, igloo, existence. The hardship, shared, somehow never felt so hard.

# YASMIN ALIBHAI-BROWN

*Yasmin Alibhai-Brown was born in Kampala, Uganda. She is a journalist, author, and broadcaster who has won numerous awards for her journalism.*

My family in Uganda was not rich. We were poor, though never as poor as black Africans. We lived in a succession of flats. The home I most remember was the flat in town, on Allidina Visram Street, where I lived for the first eight years of my life. Allidina Visram was an Asian pioneer, businessman, and philanthropist. Our flat was above the marketplace, had one bedroom, a dark kitchen, and bathroom which was a room with a tap and bucket. It was painted a horrible, bright green and the sofa was green, too. A small cupboard with a glass door showed off school prizes and had a replica of the Kaaba, the sacred site in Mecca. My much older brother and sister slept in the sitting room.

There were three other flats along the corridor. Other Asian families lived there. Two were Hindu, one was Sunni Muslim. We were Shia Muslims. But they were family, sometimes closer to me, and more protective than my own. I was the youngest, born ten years after my sister. My mother had a hard life. She sewed clothes for people, cooked for weddings, and taught children in the local nursery school. I slept between my mum and dad till I was twelve. But we had visitors drop in every day – mostly women who had been to the market – and, at lunchtime, food would be shared between the four families. Doors were always open, Bollywood songs would be played all day and the children played in the corridors or downstairs, near the market, where we would buy mangos sprinkled with salt and chilli powder.

I can still see my mum sitting down on the kitchen floor rolling chapatis and cooking them on a Primus stove. And her singing lovely songs as she washed my hair as I sat on a wooden stool in the bathroom. My parents did not get on, and on those days and nights when the rows between them got too bad, she took us to one of the neighbours who comforted and looked after us. This was a community of kindness. We moved to a bigger house with a garden but never found such a community again.

I visited the flat when I returned to Uganda in 1999. It was derelict. They had changed the name of the street. After Asians were expelled from Uganda by Idi Amin, they wiped us out of history, too. My heart broke.

# AMELIA BULLMORE

*Amelia Bullmore was born in Chelsea, London, and is an actress and writer for stage and screen. She has had many television roles, including playing Steph Barnes in* Coronation Street *and DCI Gill Murray in* Scott & Bailey.

The house I was born in and grew up in (1964-1976) is a tall house in London. At the time, lorries lumbered past and a sign at the end of the street pointed to Brighton. I thought if I walked for half an hour I'd be by the sea. The road has since been narrowed at one end and is almost unrecognisably smart.

The attic housed a lodger usually, sometimes an au-pair girl. Bedrooms were on the middle floors. The hub was the basement, which contained a kitchen, playroom, larder and what you'd now call a utility room. The playroom was a big, low-ceilinged, lino-floored room, which sometimes doubled as a dining room if my mum and dad had a lot of people for dinner. It had doors to the coal hole out front, a fire, a piano, and a huge cupboard containing toys, games, and art and craft stuff. The cupboard had red resin knobs. Just thinking about it makes me excited. It was extremely well stocked by my mother. Copydex, string, corrugated cardboard, scraps, paper, things that might come in handy for collage and construction. There must have been a box of oil pastels in there because I remember my brother and I colouring in the grooves of a radiator with them. The colour went on like a dream, gliding on to the hot metal. Mum, understandably, went mad. I was a very poor student of the piano and was amazed no one before me had thought of writing the notes on the keys to make things easier. Mum, understandably, went mad.

We had a record player down there and some singles – Beach Boys, The Beatles – were coloured. The bright red disc would spin round and we'd 'skate' on the lino, gripping wooden building blocks under our feet. This game was called Skating, Skating Tra-la-la. I also remember a brilliant game of doctors when our white coats were spattered with cherry juice blood.

If Mum and Dad had entertained the night before, we descended for breakfast hoping for scraps from the abandoned dining table. Stale French bread, grapes and, ideally, cheesecake.

I think of that house and the time I spent in it as more or less perfect.

# AMANDA LAMB

*Amanda Lamb is a television presenter and former model. Born in Portsmouth, Amanda is best known for presenting* A Place in the Sun.

I can still vividly remember moving into what I fondly think of as my childhood home. I was three years old and my brother was still a baby. I can remember my mother opening the front door and letting me run in and explore all the rooms. Everything was new and sparkling and I was so excited. We had been given a brand new council house in a cul-de-sac full of families similar to ours. The cul-de-sac was missing a house. There was no number 13; the builders were apparently superstitious, so where number 13 should have been became the place where, when we got older, all of the kids would congregate to play British Bulldog and practise our handstands.

Our house was always filled with love and laughter and a menagerie of various pets: rabbits, guinea pigs, a goldfish called Lazurus, budgies, canaries, tortoises, and the most wonderful dog that grew up with us all. It was the place the whole family gathered to be together and share happy times. My grandparents lived close by and they were there every weekend. We had a magical upbringing and did lots of things that I try to replicate with my own children now; things like den building under the dining table, treasure hunts, picnics, and paddling pools in the back garden on those all so rare hot summer days. As I grew older and became an awkward teenager it became a place of refuge, where I would mope around for days when the hormones were raging. Or I would find myself sitting on the bottom stair near the telephone willing for it to ring and that the boy I'd fallen madly in love with would be calling to ask me to the ball!

Mostly though, it was my sanctuary. It saw me through the best of times and the worst of times. It sheltered and protected us all and I can never think about it without smiling fondly.

I left home when I was twenty-one and, with knapsack over my shoulder, headed to London, where the streets where paved with gold and the rest, as they say, is history; but my family home with its abundance of memories, magic, and love, never strays far from my thoughts.

# Nicholas Parsons CBE

*Nicholas Parsons is an actor, radio and television presenter. He is best known for hosting* Sale of the Century *and* Just a Minute. *He received an Officer of the Order of the British Empire in 2004 and was promoted to Commander of the Order of the British Empire in 2014 for charitable services.*

The house where I was born is in Grantham, Lincolnshire. It was a late-Victorian building on the corner of Castlegate overlooking The Green. I have discovered that in your memory places from your childhood are always larger than their actual size. I discovered this when I returned to Grantham as an adult. My family left there when I was aged eight. The Green that was huge in my childhood memory as I watched the hunt assemble from an upstairs window was actually very small. My father was a doctor in a country practice with two partners. He had a waiting room and surgery on the ground floor of the house. Although he was only a family doctor, he earned enough money to employ what were called domestic servants, but money went much further then. We even had a nanny for a few years. She was a lovely person and I adored her. She was from a nearby village of Swayfield, where her brothers, Ernest and Percy, ran a builder's business. Her father worked on the railway and I loved staying with them, enjoying the simple country pleasures to which they introduced me, such as picking cowslips and Nanny's Mummy, as we called her, making cowslip wine. I still dream about her Yorkshire pudding. She served it as a starter to the meal and poured the juices from the joint she was cooking over it.

Nanny's name was Nellie Kettle and she looked after my older brother, myself and younger sister with a natural skill, amazing efficiency and huge love, with apparently no training. She came as a young eighteen-year-old and stayed for seven years until she left to marry Joe Cox from her same village, who often visited us in the nursery. He was a trained masseur.

How delightfully simple and safe life was in those days in the late 1920s, when very few people had cars but most villages as well as towns were served by an amazing rail network. This all disappeared in the 1960s when Mr Beeching was engaged to simplify the railway system. Nanny often took us to the station in Grantham. How I loved the atmosphere and excitement of travelling. The huge steam engine was so impressive, I decided that was what I wanted to do when I grew up: become an engine driver! When we arrived at Swayfield, the guard helped us by carrying our cases to the exit. Everyone was so much more at ease with life and each other. The pressure of life today has taken all of this away. Outside the station in Swayfield, Joe's father had left one of his horses harnessed to a cart from their farm. We all got into the cart and sat down. Nanny took the reins, gave them a flick, and the lovely white cart horse trotted off and took us without any apparent guidance to Mr Cox's farm. There was nothing on the road and the horse knew the route by instinct. We just took it all for granted. It was enjoyable and completely safe. We then walked from the farm to her mother's home. I can picture it all now as if it was yesterday.

There are many stories and vivid memories from that period of my young life, but perhaps the one about the train and the horse and life in a small village, all stemming from the house where I was born, illustrates a way of life that has disappeared but where the memory sustains me and gives one pleasure to recall.

# Tracie Bennett

*Tracie Bennett was born in Leigh, Lancashire. She is a stage and television actress who has received Olivier Awards for her performances in musicals and her television credits include* Coronation Street, Going Out *and* Scott & Bailey.

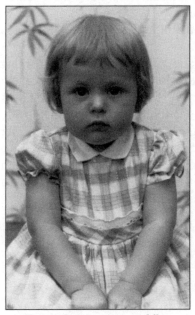

*Tracie Bennett as a toddler.*

When I was a child, about two years old, the family lived in a large house in the country up-north.

The kitchen was exceedingly large but always cold, so my parents had a smokeless-fuel stove installed. There was a large supply of coal in the back garden shed, so my father decided one snowy night to use the coal up until a stock of smokeless-fuel could be bought. For some weeks we all enjoyed the warmth and cosiness of the kitchen. During this time, we were given a collie dog. The dog had a vicious nature; he had been well trained as a guard dog but, strangely, the dog hated men. I remember it all so well!

Weirdly, my sisters and I loved him. His name was Rocky and he was a collie crossed with a spaniel type; he was almost a sheep dog and he was black and white.

On one occasion, it was freezing cold day. The dog wouldn't

let my father back into the house after Dad had gone outside to get a coal shovel for our fire. Blizzard-like snow was falling heavily. When he eventually managed to get back into the house after spending hours outside, my parents decided that, the next day the dog would be returned to its previous owner. We all begged them not to do it, because we loved him even though we had only had him a few weeks or so.

After stoking up the stove in order to keep the house warm overnight, we all retired to bed. At about 3 a.m. the dog began barking non-stop at the bottom of the stairs. My father got up to see just what the problem with the dog was.

Dad was horrified to find thick smoke everywhere, which was pouring out of the stove. He opened the doors and then poured water on the burning coals of the stove.

The coal had clogged the outlet pipe with soot and prevented smoke from passing through it.

From that day on, only smokeless-fuel was used. But for that dog, we would have all died that night from smoke inhalation.

Nevertheless, and sadly for my sisters and I, the dog was returned to its owner. It's strange to think that without that lovely vicious dog being in our house for a minimal amount of time, not one of us would have survived that night.

I know I was only two, but I remember everything so well and that's why I was one of the first people in London to have a smoke alarm fitted in the first flat that I bought in 1979.

Bless Rocky!

# LIZ FRASER

*Liz Fraser is an author, broadcaster and journalist. She is also a radio presenter, a columnist and a frequent commentator on* This Morning, Sky News *and numerous other current-affair programmes.*

I lived in the same house in Oxford from the age of four to the day I left home when I was eighteen.

It was just a very ordinary, bay-fronted house in a quiet, residential street conveniently near to a huge hospital. I was extremely accident-prone as a child, so we made many dashes from my house to A&E!

For such an unassuming street, it has housed some exciting residents.

J.R.R. Tolkien lived there when he wrote *The Lord of the Rings*, and the comedian and writer David Mitchell lived down the road when I was there.

I had a massive crush on him when I was about seven. I used to run along the road and hide behind a tree until he walked to school, so I could watch him. Probably best you don't tell him this.

Oh, and Doris and Brian lived at no. 72. So it was *all go*.

This was the 1980s and 1990s, so we had a telephone in the hall, a VHS player in the lounge, and a soda-stream machine in the kitchen.

The main object in the lounge was a grand piano, which I played for about two hours a day, and also used as a launch pad for various ballet twirls and spins, while listening to music very loudly.

I'm sure my parents loved this.

My bedroom was upstairs, at the end of what I always thought was a very long corridor, but was probably actually only about three paces. Everything seems so much bigger when you're a child.

I had a built-in high sleeper made of pine, with a ladder at one end, and my desk was underneath it, facing the wall. I had the Periodic Table on the wall, and a map of the world on my desk.

I *loved* it under there.

Quiet, secret, cosy and undistracted. I did all my A-level revision there, very happily.

Every morning I would lie in bed listening to the coo-coo-coo of the wood pigeon in the tall pine tree outside my window.

I once had to try and climb in through that window using a *huge* ladder that I carried out from the garage, after a somewhat un-sober evening in one of Oxford's watering holes ... where I lost my house keys.

When my parents sold the house, I didn't go back to help them pack up and move; I feel bad about this, but I was so attached to the building, the walls, the furniture exactly as it was, the shadows and light, the sounds and smells of my childhood there, that I couldn't bear to see it changed in any way.

I couldn't even remember what it looked like, for a long time. It was as if I had locked it all away, when the house was sold.

I've been past it in recent years for the first time since 1992, and I almost can't recognize it. The two huge trees in the front have been cut down, changing the whole feel of the house, for me. It doesn't feel like the same place.

For years, I couldn't remember what the house looked like inside.

Then recently I had a complete nervous breakdown, and I suddenly had the most incredibly vivid memories of every room in the house that I'd never been able to access before. It was like opening a box to a thousand memories that had been locked away, and actually standing in the house, touching the walls, sitting in the kitchen, running down the garden. It was very strange ... but lovely to be able to go back into the house I grew up in, and visit it again, in my mind.

And now that I've remembered it, I can go back again any time.

# TRACY-ANN OBERMAN

*Tracy-Ann Oberman is an actress, playwright and writer. She is famed for her role as Chrissie Watts in* Eastenders. *Tracy-Ann contributes articles to newspapers and magazines and writes radio plays for BBC Radio 4.*

The house I spent my formative years in was in Stanmore, Middlesex, at the far end of the Jubilee Line on the London Tube. I always liked the Jubilee Line. In those days it was the shiny new silver line; it had regal connotations and to be at the end of it felt suburban, but important. Our house was a new build. My mum had grown up in East Finchley, a stone's long throw from the prestigious Kenwood House in beautiful Hampstead Heath. Having two little girls by the time she was twenty-one, our small top-floor flat in Dollis Hill soon grew far too small to house us and our 'troubled' mongrel rescue dog, Lucky.

So my dad told my mum to leave it to him, and bought our new house, off plan, in Stanmore, Middlesex. The day we moved in I was three-and-a-half and I remember drawing up in the family's red Cortina. My mum took one look at our new square house and burst into tears. It looked like a child's drawing of a house: a box with four windows and a door. Once inside, her tears turned to sobs. The house looked nothing as it had looked in the sales picture. Soulless rooms with no character. It was also paper thin. If you sneezed in the upstairs bedroom, it could be heard crystal clear anywhere downstairs. Privacy was a no-no. Every private conversation had to be made in hushed tones or sign language. Imagine trying to conduct a teenage phone call with a boyfriend under those conditions. Nightmare!

My bedroom had purple curtains and a bed and a desk. I was privileged. My sister's bedroom was like a narrow cell. With no window gifting natural light, it was just big enough to fit a solitary single bed. But to my sister and I this new house felt like a palace. No longer sharing a room, we became very territorial over our space and belongings. And we did have a garden, with a death-trap wobbly climbing frame, and neighbouring little sisters on the other side of the fence, Natasha and Michelle, who became our friends.

Oh, and we had an avocado-coloured bathroom suite. I still remember lying in that avocado bath, aged thirteen, listening to David Bowie's *Hunky Dory* on the family tape recorder and my mind exploding and expanding with creative wonder and possibilities.

The house also had a dining room. This felt very posh; a walnut modernist dining table and matching chairs and light brown walls. This room was slated for adults only; with a drinks trolley, ice bucket, carefully positioned large glass ashtrays, a Lazy Susan and a stereo system that would occasionally blast out Donna Summer or the Rolling Stones late into the night ... It was a strictly cordoned-off VIP room. It smelt of furniture polish and cigarette smoke. And reverberated with the sounds of heated political debates and bursts of laughter.

My mum may have hated it and put it on the market where it remained for seventeen years, but we all loved it. It was our house and my memories are still vivid. Alphabetti spaghetti on brown toast for tea after school in our small brown kitchen with the pull-down table. Smarty Arty parties in the garden for my birthday. My sister and I playing some weird game we'd invented called Yogi Boo Boo Bear that we fought about for hours in the gap under the stairs. Pretending I was an astronaut (aged four) and sliding down the bannisters and breaking my arm. Tweetie the Budgie in his giant cage. The fateful night when over dinner, Lucky, our beloved rescue mutt, stared malevolently at bald Uncle Edwin and then suddenly out of nowhere took a chunk out of his leg. Lucky disappeared the next day to go and 'live on a farm'.

A family life was pieced together in that house. Deaths, births, marriages, triumphs and despairs. Nursery school to first day at university. First love and broken hearts. Entertaining ... lots of entertaining. A community of young couples and their kids that bonded as a new family, and one we are all still close to today. It may have been an imperfect house but it was a glue that held us all together.

# Samantha Giles

*Samantha Giles was born in Maidstone, Kent. She is a television and stage actress, best known for her role as Bernice Blackstock in* Emmerdale.

I still dream about our childhood home, even though my parents moved to Wales when I was in my twenties. It's somehow imbedded in the depths of my unconscious – the through-lounge with the chintzy silver sofas, the rugs scattered everywhere, the framed watercolour pictures squashed in random designs on every wall. My bedroom – a black cobweb shawl draped 'artistically' on the wall, and, always, matching wallpaper and curtains which I now cringe at the memory of.

I have always been afraid of the dark and as a child I used to insist on the landing light being kept on. Every night my dad would turn it off when he went to bed at 10 p.m. sharp, and I would wait patiently until my parents were asleep and then creep out and switch it back on, knowing I could then fall into a safe slumber.

I was only very young (around twelve years of age) when I decided to read Dennis Wheatley's *The Devil Rides Out* (ironically my on-screen father Patrick Mower starred in the film version of this). I read the entire book in a day, drinking up the plot with a mixture of fascination and fear. My fervour for it gained momentum when my parents told me that the writer had actually become embroiled in the satanic cult during his research, so it became almost impossible for him to escape. Of course I hadn't bargained on the fact that later that evening I would be sitting on the landing crying my eyes out, terrified to go to sleep, as images of devils with burning red eyes and long fingernails would haunt my room.

# Marc Baylis

*Marc Baylis was born in Stourport-on-Severn, Worcestershire. He is a stage, television, and film actor. He is best known for his role as Rob Donovan in* Coronation Street.

As a child, Tuesday evenings meant that my father would be dealt the task of trying to manage my sister, Natasha, and I by himself. My mother would be enjoying 'me time' teaching her weekly dance class.

This particular winter's evening was going quite smoothly. He had given us the task of weighing bags of sweets for him to sell the next day in his shop: a child's dream! Yes, my family sold sweets and, yes, sweets would leap into my mouth at every given opportunity. Once the sugar rush was beginning to subside it was time to get ready for bed. This is where the trouble began.

Natasha and I always used to warm our pyjamas by the fire in the living room. The race was on to claim the warmest spot on the hearth, which I frustratingly didn't win on this occasion. Never to be scuppered as a child, after my sister had smugly gone back upstairs and my dad briefly left the room, I had a brainwave! Why not put my pyjamas on the metal grid that protects us from the fire? They will get really toasty there.

Whoosh! Up in flames they go.

'Fire!' I yelled, while yanking them off the metal grid and onto the carpet, which is also pretty flammable. Natasha simultaneously decides to bounce head first down the stairs in sheer panic and my father is dealt the conundrum of either extinguishing the fire or aiding my contorted sister.

My mother returned home to discover my sister sprawled on the sofa with a bag of peas on her head, my father nursing a whisky to calm his nerves, and me trimming the carpet to hide any evidence.

Thankfully we all lived happily ever after ... roll on next Tuesday!

# DEENA PAYNE

*Deena Payne was born in Orpington, Kent. She is an actress on stage and television, most famous for her long-running role in* Emmerdale.

*Deena sniffing sweet peas in her garden.*

When asked to think back to my childhood, the first thing that springs to mind is the garden at our first home. Gardening runs in the family; my grandparents on both sides of the family were avid gardeners and I have never had a home without a garden.

Every season of the year holds a precious memory; in spring I can remember Dad holding me up to see the blackbird's nest in the hawthorn hedge and the amazement I felt at seeing the blue-speckled eggs hatching into tiny birds, constantly twittering for food. In summer: helping Dad mow the lawn, being thrown on top of the grass cuttings in the wheelbarrow and him running down the garden to dump the whole contents on the compost heap, me included! It was a garden so full of colour, and gorgeous scents from roses and lavender. My father would cut blooms and give me them to bring to class. I clearly recall walking to school with a huge bunch of garden flowers for the classroom. There were lovely birthday parties in the garden at the end of August when we played games. Then autumn was spent digging and watching the robin search for worms.

I loved being outdoors and when I wasn't doing my dance classes I would be at the local stable with my best friend Glynis, helping out and hoping for a free ride (probably being more of a pest!). I can still remember the names of the ponies, even though it was over fifty years ago: Squiby, Pippin, Cloudy, Star.

I have very industrious parents, always creating, working, going to evening classes, and I think I've taken a lot of that on too. I used to have a tiny cooking set, including a rolling pin, and used to copy my mother making pastry. I made my first stew when I was eight. Mum was poorly and shouted instructions from upstairs, but because I was so tiny I had to get a step seat to climb up to the cooker so I could see.

I felt very grown up when I caught the no. 61 bus to Orpington ... on my own! I rehearsed 'tuppenny half return please' for ages beforehand.

Mum used to take me into Orpington to shop. I loved the shops where there were purses and leather bags, and stationery shops: I loved the smells. We used to go for lunch at a café up a winding staircase; it was typical late-1950s, brown colours, lino flooring, but the steak and kidney pie and mash was to die for!

The more I think back the more I remember, but these few memories should be enough for now.

# LISA JEWELL

*Lisa Jewell is an author, born in London. Her first novel* Ralph's Party *became the best-selling debut novel of 1999 and her subsequent novels have all been* Sunday Times *bestsellers.*

I grew up in a rambling cottage in one of the furthest corners of north London, right at the very tip of a Tube line. We had fields behind our house and a village shop at the bottom of the garden path, yet we were just half an hour away from the West End. It was a strange hybrid of city and country life and I always found the contrast a little bit frustrating, so tantalisingly close to the action, yet so irritatingly far. I lived there from birth until I left home at the age of seventeen.

The house grew with us as a family, from a tiny two-up two-down sliver with a bathroom off the kitchen, to a four-up three-down after my second sister arrived, and then finally, a four-up four-down with a conservatory, built very badly over the course of a long hot summer by a Mr Paddam, who brought us curry in Tupperware, cooked by his wife. Our next-door neighbours were a silver-haired old couple, called Bill and Margaret Mayhew, who had an outside toilet and a tin bath. We shared a party line with them well into the 1980s.

Mr Henderson ran the village shop at the end of the path. I'm sure he stocked a very wide range of produce, from newspapers to washing powder, but all I can remember is Wagon Wheels. My sisters and I weren't allowed chewing gum, so once we sneaked into Mr Henderson's shop and bought a packet. We chewed it up, stick by stick, really, really quickly and spat it out of our bedroom window onto the roof of the kitchen below. When Mr Henderson retired in the late 1970s the shop was sold, and converted into a regular house, and we spent much more time in our mother's car driving up and down the road to Waitrose.

*Lisa Jewell, left, enjoying the swings with her mother, sister and puppy.*

My parents were incredibly sociable and glamorous. Our front door was always open and our house was the venue for regular, shockingly debauched, and drunken dinner parties that went on until the early hours. We'd be wheeled down the stairs in our nighties at the start of the party to kiss everyone goodnight and then wheeled back up again. Once a naked man crashed into our room and tried to go to sleep in the airing cupboard.

When we were small, Sacha and I shared a bedroom together. We would jump up and down on our beds for hours after lights out, singing pop songs and making up long, convoluted stories. I moved into the front bedroom when the extension was built. My parents redecorated all the bedrooms in floor-to-ceiling Laura Ashley. Mine was pink. Pink wallpaper, pink curtains, pink borders.

Eventually I moved into the attic room (blue Laura Ashley) where I spent my teenage years listening to John Peel, writing to weird and wonderful pen pals all over the country, drawing pencil sketches of Morrissey, and contemplating suicide. I once swallowed ten paracetamols after reading in my sister's diary that she thought I looked like an old tramp in my grandfather's overcoat. But by the time I left home in 1988 I was happy and confident and ready to take on the world.

I didn't look back as I packed my trunk and headed down south to art college in Epsom. I'd had an idyllic, carefree childhood and I thought that life would always be this easy. It was two weeks before my twenty-first birthday that the unblemished idyll of my childhood suffered an irrevocable fissure. I was living in Battersea. I'd spent the day there with my middle sister and that evening we drove across London, with my boyfriend James, for a barbecue with my parents. My little sister was still living at home. We sat in the conservatory, drinking beer and eating meat. My mother looked extraordinarily slim and when I commented on this she said, 'There's a reason why I'm so thin. Ask your father.' So I did. And he told us that he was in love with someone else, that he was leaving, that it was over. It was a shocking revelation. My parents had the strongest marriage of any of their friends. To hear that he'd had an affair, that he didn't want to live in our home with our mother anymore was unthinkable. But at the time all I can really remember thinking was, oh God, how could you have done this in front of James?

I never really thought of the cottage as my home after that evening. For a while after my father left it became a hang-out for all our friends. I'd actually leave my flatshare in Battersea every weekend to stay at my mum's because it was more fun! But eventually it quietened down and the cottage just became the place where my mum lived, unhappily, alone.

When it was sold in 2002, I didn't feel sad. I saw it as a positive thing that my mum was finally moving on, but sadly, only a year after she moved out she was diagnosed with lung cancer. She died in May 2015 at the age of sixty-one. Coming back to the house I never thought I'd see again was even more poignant than it might already have been. The cottage hadn't been very well maintained while we lived there so I'd assumed that it would be unrecognisable now that it was owned by a young family. What amazed me was how little had changed. The ramshackle porch was still there, rotten wood and all. And so was Mr Paddam's shonky conservatory, patched up with plastic sheeting, and in danger of imminent collapse. They've yet to replace my mum's lovingly maintained 1970s orange Formica and stripped pine kitchen or to repaint the plum walls in the dining room. It felt just like walking into the childhood home I remembered. I half-expected to see our family photos in frames on the windowsill where they used to be.

Upstairs, the Laura Ashley was gone but the sticky pads on the door where the plaque that said 'Lisa's Room' had been were still there. But most exciting of all was the package that the owners had found hidden away at the bottom of my mum's wardrobe. It was an envelope stuffed full of black and white photos of my mother and father in their courting days, young and beautiful, and madly in love. There were bundles of love letters and four of my mother's diaries, tiny black leather ones, embossed with her initials. They covered the years 1964 to 1967. I pored through them feverishly and there it was in my mother's own words, her love affair with my father, 'I am completely infatuated!!!' There are entries about the cottage too, 'I cooked a rabbit curry while Anthony painted the ceiling'; and their engagement, 'A. proposed! I accepted! I love him!' And reading these diaries underneath the apple trees in the garden I was suddenly filled with the sense of what this place meant to me. Not, as I'd felt for so long, just the place where my parents had split up, but the place where they'd fallen in love, where they'd created a home, and made their dreams come true. This was the place where it had all started, a long time before me, my sisters, our lives, our children. This was a place not just of endings, but of beginnings, and I'm so very grateful that I got a chance to go back and remind myself of that.

# PARADISE LOST

My mother was the one who found and fell in love with the house. She often recalled that a lovely feeling came over her when she first entered it, as though the house had greeted her with a welcoming embrace. The house exuded an air of peace and happiness. In her search for the perfect residence, she had viewed many homes alone while my father was at work, but found that many had unpleasant atmospheres. One in particular she recalled held such a feeling of pure evil that the hairs on the back of her neck stood on end, and she turned and ran out. But this house was different.

'Hasn't this house got a lovely atmosphere!' was a comment that was to be made by many visitors in the years to come.

The house was built in around 1900; three families have lived in it since its creation. I know little about the first residents, other than that some letters were found in the attic written from a soldier to his mother during the First World War. The son of the second inhabitants now stood on the doorstep before me, apparently yearning to re-enter, and the third family were my own parents and their motley crew.

My mum lost her beloved mother at the tender age of thirteen and wasn't terribly close to her father, a disciplinarian schoolteacher with a penchant for whisky. As soon as they were able, she and her younger sister began to make their own way in the world.

Mum was a nineteen-year-old singer when she met my father in the Plaza Ballroom in Belfast in 1946. He was a professional musician with his own Glenn Miller-type orchestra, playing in venues around Northern Ireland. It was love at first sight. On their first meeting, my father jokingly asked, in what he thought was a Clarke Gable manner, 'How would you like to be married to me, kid?'

Several months later, she was!

Mum was keen to create the kind of family home she had yearned for, but never known, following the premature death of her mother. She gave birth to three children in quite quick succession after her marriage, two boys and a girl. By the time mum had me she was almost forty. There was quite an age gap between my siblings and I. My older brother was seventeen when I was born, my other brother was thirteen, and my sister was eleven. My late arrival caused my mother to refer to me for the rest of her life as her 'last rose of summer', a phrase I didn't fully understand until I too was blessed with a little rosebud on the cusp of my forties.

Growing up in our house in the 1970s and 1980s is nothing short of bliss to recall. We were a big, tight, family unit. Even when both brothers got married in the 1970s, they brought their wives to live in our family home. The first grandchild also started his life here.

The house seemed huge when I was a child and had plenty of nooks and crannies for my Alsatian puppy and I to hide in. There were beautiful fireplaces in every reception room and bedroom with a bell beside each one to call the maid. The bell system in the hall indicated which room was calling for service. It was all quite *Downton Abbey*, but my father, in an attempt to drag the house into the 1970s, ripped all these lovely features out of the house. Our 1970s house décor was mostly orange, yellow, and brown, very psychedelic suburbia!

My favourite pastime was to lay some old net curtains on the hall stairs from top to bottom and slide down them on my bottom. It was fantastic! I felt like a speeding bullet! I also loved sliding down the banisters and using my parents' bed as a trampoline. It was so springy I would bounce up high then land on my back in hysterical giggles. My dog loved to join in the bouncing fun, too.

I spent long sunny days riding my bike, jumping on my space hopper and climbing the trees in our garden, then hanging from the branches by my ankles. It was an idyllic childhood in that big, old house filled with love and laughter. The memory of my mother's home cooking still makes my mouth water and me yearn for the days of her homemade apple pies and rhubarb tarts, both crafted with fare from our garden. She'd serve up big gut-busting Ulster fry-ups on plates so huge we referred to them as 'bin lids' and Sunday roasts with melt-in-the-mouth beef, the like of which I have never tasted since. Mum's Christmas dinners were also legendary! Meal times were some of the best times in our house.

My parents were extremely loving; their family was their lives and I never felt anything other than adored and cherished by them. They also doted on each other. Dad made a good living with his own furniture company and we wanted for nothing. We enjoyed fabulous holidays abroad; Christmas was a time of eye-popping excess. Our front room would be so crammed with gifts for us all on Christmas morning, we could barely get the living room door open! We had a little summer house in Ballywater, a beautiful seaside town, and enjoyed trips there when the mood would take us, bundling into cars, and forming a family convoy all the way. Various friends of my siblings would tag along. On the way we'd play those big old-fashioned eight-track cassettes on the car stereo and sing along to the Eagles, Carol King, The Beatles and Leonard Cohen. Though the song that always evokes memories for me of those sunny days in the 1970s is Mungo Jerry's 'In the Summertime', and the best part of the trip was stopping for a '99' in an Italian ice cream shop.

Even though I grew up in the midst of the troubles in Belfast, life was good. Bombs, soldiers, and police on the streets were part of everyday life back then in Ulster. I remember one evening sitting on my bed and being blown off it from the blast of a hotel around the corner being bombed. Things like this didn't faze a Belfast child. It happened all the time: bomb blasts were common in those days on the Ulster streets. I remember a van racing past our grammar school gates. Shots were being fired out the back of it at the RUC as they gave chase. Our teacher told us to get down on the floor of our classroom as they passed. We crouched down, then got up when all was clear and resumed our lesson.

When I was older, I recall being in a city centre bar with some friends. We were laughing and dancing when the DJ stopped the music and announced there was a security alert. We all cheered, took our drinks outside, and waited across the road while the premises were checked for devices. Then we piled back into the pub after the all-clear was given, totally unfazed. In another instance my friend and I were in the Europa Hotel (famed for being the most bombed hotel in Europe) when a bomb exploded in the College of Business Studies in the street opposite. We were momentarily disorientated before the band played on. They started a rendition of 'Return to Sender' which everyone found highly amusing. It might sound blasé but it's simply how we coped with the permanent threat to our safety.

Life in Ulster during those times probably seemed like a frightening existence to others. You couldn't go into a shop without having your handbag and shopping bags inspected for devices; soldiers got on every bus leaving the city centre as I travelled home from school and searched, checking for bombs. It didn't bother my friends or I; we never worried about what would happen if they found a suspicious object. When you are raised in a conflict, you don't know any differently. From the age of two until I was thirty-two, I lived through a time of great unrest, yet I have no memories of living in mortal fear, it was simply normality.

My childhood was filled with dreams of what I would be when I grew up (becoming a member of Pan's People was top of the list!) and I would spend hours play-acting with my dog. My favourite treat of the week was getting a pasty supper on a Saturday night and watching *Dad's Army*, followed by the *Generation Game* and *Starsky and Hutch*. I was madly in love with 'Hutch' and was sure I would someday be his wife. Though marriage never beckoned I did end up having contact with David Soul later in life, when he helped me with a charity project. He was lovely to me, and his mobile number still nestles in my contact list. Lovely Mr Soul aside, someone very special was soon to enter my life.

I was fourteen years old as we headed into the 1980s. By this stage, my brothers, their wives, my nephew and my aunt had moved out and the house was home to just my parents, my sister and I. Curiously, my eldest brother had moved out into the house my parents had sold to purchase our present home. He went on to raise a family in those rooms where he and my siblings had grown up.

With my siblings' departure, I finally got my own room,

which was decorated in coffee and cream, the trendy colours of the time. I had Marilyn Monroe posters and album covers on my walls. At last I had a place to dream in privacy. It became my sanctuary: I would spend hours in there writing in my Holly Hobbie diary and listening to The Undertones (my crush had changed from David Soul to Billy Doherty, The Undertones' drummer).

At the tender age of fifteen I met my destiny. I was at a fairground with my best friend Nikki when my eyes fell on a boy. I flushed red hot as my hormones awoke and were whipped into a raging tsunami of lust. I had only ever felt this way about my pin-ups before, never a real person. I couldn't take my eyes off him. As it happened, Nikki knew his friend and we went over to talk to them. His name was Steven Guy, he was seventeen, he had the obligatory 1980s moustache, was tall and gorgeous – the spitting image of the actor Tom Selleck.

Luckily the attraction was instant for him, too. We started dating and a few months later he proposed and bought me an engagement ring. I was only sixteen and my parents weren't happy. They thought our relationship was too intense and they worried about my schoolwork; I was about to sit important exams. They banned me from seeing Steven. I was distraught. My teenage heart couldn't live without him. So I developed a cunning plan and pretended I was meeting Nikki, but instead enjoyed clandestine meetings with Steven in a derelict house off the notorious Shankill Road. It was the stuff of Romeo and Juliet!

Eventually my folks got wind of our meetings and accepted we weren't a flash in the pan. They allowed us to date. For the next three years I wore Steven's engagement ring on my right hand so as not to upset my parents. It was a secret sign of our commitment.

When I was nineteen Steven proposed again and bought me another beautiful ring, but the time still wasn't right. I knew telling my parents would cause upheaval. My mother had a debilitating lung disease and had just been diagnosed with rheumatoid arthritis. She had also developed heart disease and was waiting on triple heart bypass surgery.

At my parents' request I had gone into the family furniture

business upon leaving school. There wasn't really a job there for me: I typed the odd invoice and answered the phone, but my sister was already the full-time company secretary and my brothers were employed there, too. In my heart I had always wanted to be a writer. I had dreams of having my own newspaper column someday, but the odds of that ever happening for me seemed slim. As Mum's health deteriorated my father asked me to stay at home and look after her for a while – until she had her heart surgery. A while turned into twenty years, which was the rest of my mother's life.

I was now a full-time carer. I did everything around the house and for my mother, including learning how to perform her daily physiotherapy to clear her lungs of mucus.

After Mum's surgery I kept asking my father when I would return to work but he would never reply. It was clear he wanted me to stay with Mum, and I knew she needed help: I couldn't walk away. Time passed, I looked after my mother and Steven and I made the most of what time we could manage to steal together. We enjoyed a wonderful romance through the entire decade of the 1980s. It wasn't like the moving-in-after-hello relationships of today. Our dates were always incredibly romantic, and somehow parting, at the end of the night, to go to our separate family homes, made our romance all the sweeter, but it couldn't carry on like that forever.

After ten years and two engagements rings Steven dropped a bombshell: he told me was going to work abroad. He'd been offered a job in the Seychelles and he wanted me to go with him. I could understand that he wanted to see the world. We were both still young: he was twenty-seven, I was twenty-five. But I couldn't abandon Mum. I wasn't strong enough to walk away when my mother depended on me and my father relied on me to be there for her. Sadly, Steven and I parted ways. I loved him, but I didn't want to leave my family.

He left for the Seychelles. We didn't maintain contact. I knew I'd lost the love of my life.

It was around this time that my sister got married and moved out of the house. And then there were three: mum, dad and me.

Years passed and Mum's health deteriorated. I fitted in

piecemeal work for several greeting card companies writing verses for cards around my full-time caring duties. I took a year-long correspondence course in creative writing. Then I entered a writing competition which involved penning a cinema review. The prize was to have my piece published in the *Daily Mirror* newspaper. I won and from this I acquired my own movie review column, 'Jacqueline McGregor's Cinema Hotseat' with the *Daily Mirror* for the next three years. It was a dream come true, but my other dream of becoming a wife and mother was firmly put on hold.

Mum was becoming increasingly forgetful and confused. She couldn't be trusted to do anything herself. She would do bizarre things like put her reading glasses in the fridge. She misplaced items like her hearing aid, purse, and door keys constantly. I spent most days looking for things she'd lost. She no longer remembered her children's birthdays. She couldn't concentrate on television programmes and couldn't remember what she'd just been talking about. Looking after her became harder than ever, though even with my mother's failing health my parents and I managed to lead a happy life together. We all got on well. My father was still my hero. I adored him. All my life we had been extremely close. Dad had a wonderful sense of humour. He never once raised his voice to me and was nothing other than supportive, loving, and kind. He was my rock, counsellor, and touchstone throughout my life. Dad was always there for me and I was for him.

Then Dad retired, closed his business, and we were together all the time. He was great company; we laughed a lot. The three of us went out most days for afternoon tea and shopping, and my siblings would call in and out. Mum was pleasantly confused, but happy.

We had no idea life was about to change beyond all recognition.

One evening Mum, Dad and I were quietly watching television. Suddenly, my mother sat forward in her chair, became very distressed and asked tearfully in a child-like voice, 'When is my mummy coming to collect me?' Those words were to change my family and our lives forever. This was the beginning of what was to become a living nightmare for all of us. Mum became increasingly irritated that evening, desperate to see her mother and frantic to 'go home' to a house that had been demolished decades ago. My father and I had no idea what was wrong with her and reminded her that her mother had died when she was thirteen. This was a mistake! My mother, in her demented state, was hearing this shattering news of her mother's passing for the first time. She became hysterical. Dad and I were perplexed as to what to do. We had never even heard of Alzheimer's. I rang my siblings and the doctor in desperation. It was 7.30 p.m. and I was promised a house call. The doctor eventually arrived at 9 p.m. He no doubt suspected Mum had Alzheimer's/dementia but he said nothing. He prescribed diazepam and left. An hour later Mum had forgotten about her mother and the fact that she'd just been visited by the doctor.

Mum's condition worsened at an alarmingly rapid rate. Numerous tests and surgery visits ensued. In 2002 she was finally diagnosed with vascular dementia mixed with Alzheimer's disease.

My father had always received compliments on the colour of his beautiful blue eyes. It was around this time, when he heard the fate of his beloved wife Christina, that the brilliant blue light in his eyes began to fade. It was as though his life force had been put on a dimmer switch.

Mum no longer knew that my father was her husband or that I was her daughter. We struggled desperately with my mother's care. On the advice of our GP, we got in outside help in the form of two carers who would visit at night to get Mum into her nightie and put her to bed. However, the only available time slot was 7 p.m., which was ridiculously early. Soon this 'help' became nothing more than an annoyance. After a few weeks, Dad and I were fed up with the disruption to our evening routine. It was too early for my mother to go to bed at 7 p.m., so the carers were effectively just helping her into her night attire and leaving her downstairs. One evening I saw them out, and went into the living room to find Mum sitting with her nightie on over her clothes. She had refused to put it on, so they had simply put it over her head and left. I was furious! What a waste of time for everyone involved! I cut out the home care and Dad and I soldiered on regardless, doing the best we could.

The time of day I dreaded most was teatime. My mother would experience what's known in Alzheimer's as sundowning. Fading light seems to be the trigger. Some scientists think that changes in the brain of someone with Alzheimer's affect their body clock. As the day comes to an end and tiredness creeps in, confusion and disorientation in a dementia sufferer can increase. At dusk Mum would constantly ask for her mother and question when she was going home. Every night this would happen, usually in the middle of dinner. It's understood that this may occur because the sufferer doesn't understand what is happening around them as night falls and is desperate to restore some sense of familiarity or security. Looking for a parent or a long-gone home from an earlier time in their life may be an attempt to find an environment that is familiar to them. This was one of the symptoms of my mother's disease that Dad and I found hardest to cope with, because of her agitation and distress. There was little we could do to placate her. She became a terrified child frantically searching for her mother; we simply had to wait until it passed.

Mum never recognised my father and would sometimes become very annoyed when I told her he was her husband. One night she shouted at him for almost an hour, yelling that he was an evil man for saying that he was her husband. She claimed she had never been married and threatened to call the police and have him arrested. She went on yelling at him to get out of the house. Dad just sat there in silence, trying to ignore her. He had no idea how to deal with these outbursts, neither of us had. I could see that his heart was breaking. The woman to whom he had been married for over fifty years, with whom he had had four children and nine grandchildren, didn't remember him, their marriage, or their deep love. As a passive and gentle man, entirely out of his depth, my father would simply sit, staring ahead of him, with a dazed look on his face, a little like Father Dougal from the *Father Ted* TV comedy. On these occasions I would desperately try to distract Mum.

It wasn't just my father Mum didn't remember; she had no idea who I was either. I had tried telling her she was my mother but this made her very distressed and she called me 'a wicked girl' for saying such a thing. I quickly learned to agree with anything Mum said. Keeping her calm and happy was the aim of every day. I was careful not to unleash the beast within her, but there were days when the amnesia, frustration, and confusion would become too much for her and she would explode.

Alzheimer's could make my mother's behaviour unpredictable and aggressive. My three siblings couldn't cope with my mother's illness: though they never witnessed any of her outbursts, they struggled with her changing personality. She didn't know them and they seemed to take it as a personal insult. It is a very difficult thing to come to terms with the fact that your own mother doesn't recognise you. The attention-seeking child within you can feel unimportant and rejected. On their increasingly infrequent visits I could see how uncomfortable her condition made them feel, and their hasty exits highlighted their discomfort. Our family began to fragment, though I never once felt resentment towards my siblings for their lack of involvement. They knew little of what my father and I coped with on a daily basis; Dad and I tried to shield them from it.

Mum's changing personality was also a shock to her sister when she visited after not seeing my mother for a time. My aunt offered to look after Mum while Dad and I did some shopping. I was hesitant about leaving her but my aunt was determined she could cope. When we returned from the supermarket a few hours later, my mother was standing in the back doorway arguing with my aunt. Mum was agitated and trying to leave the house. She eventually calmed down when she saw my father and I. That was the day that the severity of my mother's illness really hit my aunt. She left the house with great relief. I could see she was traumatised by my mother's aggressive behaviour. She told me later she had no idea how we coped. Frankly, neither did I!

My father and I were swept into a world of illness and isolation. I struggled terribly with my mother's illness. She wanted to be with me all the time because she felt safe with me; she was wary and suspicious of Dad. It left me with no life at all outside the dementia bubble. The only place that I found any support or help was online at the Alzheimer's Society Talking Point forum. Here I was able to talk anonymously to other carers who were going through the same ordeal as me. I met a man whom I nicknamed Braveheart and a woman named Sheila; these two faceless individuals gave me support, advice, and guidance and got me through the next few terrible years. I would sit up late into the night writing posts to them and waiting for replies. They were my lifeline, my counsellors, my friends. I will always be grateful for their encouraging words; we even managed to have the odd titter at our terrible situations. They are still my friends today; it has been a privilege to know them.

Alzheimer's is a monstrous disease. When a loved one is struck with it and begins to lose their identity, families struggle to cope because they lose their identity too. You are no longer the wife or daughter or grandchild to that person. My role with my mother changed. She thought I was just a nice girl who helped her get showered and dressed in the morning. She would engage in pleasant conversation with me in the same way she would have done with perhaps a nurse at a hospital. Mum had no idea I was her flesh and blood or that she had carried me inside her, given me life, and been by my side through every stage of my life. I seemed to be a great cause of curiosity to her. She would often ask if I had a boyfriend (after asking what my name was!) and liked to question me about my mother.

'What's your mummy like?' she asked me almost daily.

'She's tiny, just four-feet-ten tall. She's very pretty, with blonde hair, green eyes, and a lovely smile. She's very kind-hearted. I love her very much,' I would answer, turning away so that she couldn't see my tears, and how this terrible charade we went through constantly was tearing me apart.

She would be very pleased to hear this portrait of my mother; perhaps it gave her comfort on some level. She had once turned to my sister after I had walked out of the room and commented, 'You see that wee girl there: I love her!'

It was touching to know that my mother had strong feelings for me even though she had no idea I was her daughter. It spurred me to keep going. She still felt a connection to me, maybe not in a maternal way, but it was better than nothing.

My mother was a compassionate person. She was one of those people who would cry at sad news headlines, send money off to appeals, and try to help strangers around her who were in need. But when this disease possessed her she had moments when she could turn into a demon.

The life of a dementia carer is an extremely difficult one. You encounter situations on a daily basis that nothing can prepare you for. On more than one occasion, my mother, possessed with this vile disease, battered me.

She was tiny, but boy, could she pack a punch!

I had been making her tea one Sunday morning while my father was at church. The two of us were alone in the house. I had all the doors locked as usual with the keys in my pocket to stop her from making a break for freedom, which she attempted on an alarmingly regular basis. She had been trying the doors and become angry at finding them locked. Mum lived in her childhood head and was constantly waiting for her long-dead mother to collect her and take her home. She became incensed at being 'held prisoner' and told me God would punish me for being such a wicked girl. My stomach lurched as I knew she was going to have an 'episode'. I concentrated on making the tea, hoping I could distract her with drinking it, but as I turned to prepare it she attacked me from behind. As I held the kettle full of boiling water she began raining punches down on the back of my head and screaming at me. She didn't know what she was doing and continued to pummel me hard in the back, using me as a punch bag for all the pent-up fear and frustration inside her. I didn't know how to contain her, and all I could do was turn and run. I had to get away from her for fear of hitting her back, because part of me wanted to beat *her* to a pulp, for developing this disease, for stopping being my mother and for making my life hell. I, too, was a boiling cauldron of grief and terror at the way this disease had stolen all of our lives. I was also desperately lonely; my life was passing me by. I was now in my thirties and for the past few years I had lived and breathed Alzheimer's. I'd had a few romantic dalliances after Steven, but being a carer does nothing to enhance a romance. The truth was I was still in love with Steven, even after all these years. He was never far from my thoughts.

I ran upstairs away from mum's fury. With her rheumatoid arthritis she found it too hard to follow me. There, I cowered behind a door, curled up in the foetal position and sobbed my heart out, terrified and distressed by what had just happened. I wondered how much longer I could endure this torturous life that was devoid of even one iota of happiness.

The longer I stayed upstairs, the more afraid I became of her harming herself alone downstairs. Shakily I made my way towards her, dreading an encounter with my she-devil mother. When I got to her she was sitting down, looking tiny, and bewildered. Her face lit up with that beautiful smile she always displayed when I entered the room.

'When is my mummy coming to collect me?' she asked in a small, child-like voice.

'Soon,' I reassured her. 'Cup of tea?' I asked, waving a packet of chocolate biscuits at her as a distraction.

'Yes, please.'

She nodded with delight at the Hobnobs and began playing with her wedding and engagement rings, an activity she kept up most of the day. If she wasn't playing with her rings she was unpacking and packing the contents of her handbag. She was frequently very concerned about money and I always made sure there was plenty of change and some notes in her purse to make her feel more secure.

Alzheimer's also gave Mum hallucinations. She would frequently see rats sitting on the chairs. She didn't recognise her own reflection in mirrors and would become upset by the strange woman looking at her. Then there was the man that she claimed was standing in front of her staring at her. Of course there was no one there, but in my fragile mental state I found myself becoming spooked by this. My imagination began to go wild with the possibilities of who this might be, a ghost perhaps? Isolation, grief, and exhaustion can play strange tricks on people's minds. Just like my mother, I wasn't in a good place mentally or emotionally and, when I thought life couldn't get any worse, it did.

The constant stress of coping with Mum's condition led me to experience the sudden onset of panic attacks. These weren't just a little bit of anxiety: these were a full-blown feeling of terror, accompanied by violent shaking, inability to breathe properly, pins and needles in my arms, and an overwhelming need to run and keep running. The first time I had one I thought I was having a heart attack. Eventually, the panic and anxiety made me agoraphobic. I became petrified to leave the house without my father with me. Each day I would wake up with overwhelming disappointment that I had woken up at all.

With these horrible anxiety problems and a demented mother to care for, life was simply an endurance test. I told my mother's CPN (community psychiatric nurse) that I thought I was having a breakdown. She replied, 'Well, if you have a breakdown your mum will be taken into care and you hardly want that. Get your family to help.' Then she told me that she was off on a hen do and wished me a nice weekend. I soon learned that no one is interested in caring for the carer. In many cases family and friends try to ignore your plight for fear of upsetting the equilibrium. They don't want to get involved in case any help offered will become a permanent expectation. There's a lot of gratitude and platitudes but no real concern for your wellbeing. You are the willing horse, and that's the way people would like it to stay.

Then out of the blue a letter fell onto the doormat. I opened it with curiosity, it was handwritten, and post-marked Scotland. As I read it, my legs gave way beneath me. I fell onto a chair and began to weep uncontrollably. It was from Steven.

'I've never forgotten you. I still love you.'

He was working in Scotland and was due home at the weekend. He wanted to meet me for a drink. As much as I wanted to see him I knew I couldn't. It had been fourteen years since he'd left. We'd had no contact. He had no idea about the mess of a life I was leading. How could I ever explain to him about my panic attacks and the fact that I had agoraphobia? How could you tell someone you were afraid to go outside the house? He'd think I was a nutcase! I emailed him telling him that there was no point in meeting, that nothing was going to happen between us and he should forget me. Thankfully, Steven took no notice and came to see me anyway. The spark between us was still there. I explained everything to him about Mum's Alzheimer's and my panic attacks and agoraphobia. He wasn't in the least bit put off.

'I'll help you through this,' he said. 'I lost you once; I'm not going to lose you again.' I felt a huge weight lift off me. I wasn't alone anymore. I had the love of my life back and, for some insane reason, he wanted to be with me, agoraphobia, demented mother, and all.

It was due to his love and support that I was able to make it through all that was to come. He took my hand and led me through the wilderness.

Mum continued to deteriorate. Her GP thought it would be a good idea for her to go into an assessment unit to see what could be done for her, and to give Dad and I a break. We agreed. Essential building work was being carried out to our home and the dust, disruption, and dirt would have been detrimental to my mother's lung condition (bronchiectasis) and also to her mental state. This proved to be one of the darkest times of my life and my father's. The unit wasn't really equipped to deal with my mother's physical condition. A physiotherapist had to be brought in to monitor her lung disease. My father and I visited every day; we were both trained in carrying out her physio which we would do during visits.

There were seven people in the unit, many in their most disruptive stages of Alzheimer's disease. There was a lot of shouting, and it was a job getting in and out of the place as there was always one or more residents attempting the great escape when you opened the door. One gentleman, a giant of a man who had been a bouncer, would stand in the doorway of my mother's room staring menacingly at her. It scared the life out of me and it must have petrified her when we weren't there.

Building work at the house was a nightmare to endure; Dad and I continued to live in it. The house had been in a terrible state. All the windows were being replaced, the kitchen ceiling was being repaired, damp proofing work was going on, and we were changing from an oil to a gas boiler. The work went on for almost six months. During this time in the unit, my mother had been prescribed neuroleptic drugs (a tranquilizer used to treat psychotic conditions when a calming effect is desired). My mother was like a rag doll, no longer communicating when we visited, and sat staring ahead, her eyes glazed, or she would be in a heavy sleep. These drugs made the job of the carer for those in the unit easier. There were seven people in this assessment unit being looked after by one inexperienced carer, who must have experienced Mum's episodes of rage, prompting the doctor to introduce sedation.

Dad and I did our best to spur on the builders and as soon as our house was inhabitable enough we brought my mother out of the unit. She had been there four months. We had even had our Christmas dinner in there together on Christmas Day. And on that same day Steven had presented me with a third engagement ring!

On getting Mum home, I took her off the sedation drugs and she returned to being pleasant, able to converse, and happy again. Her mad rages had ceased. Unfortunately, the drugs had worsened her lung condition greatly as she had not been lucid enough in the unit to work with us or the physiotherapist to help expel the excess mucus build up from her lungs. I had a very helpful GP and she quickly got oxygen installed in our home to help Mum breathe, and from then on Mum was kept on continuous oxygen, having to wear permanent nasal cannula. We were also instructed to buy a nebuliser machine which my mother used daily. Mum's rheumatoid arthritis had become so bad that each night my father and I would have to carry her upstairs between us. We had tried having Mum and Dad sleep downstairs but she wouldn't settle and wanted to go upstairs at night.

I went to my Member of Parliament, Nigel Dodds. He helped me get a through-the-floor lift put in to make it easier for my mother to get upstairs. A stair lift wouldn't be given to her because of her dementia. I made a complaint against the assessment unit about their introduction of neuroleptic drugs in addition to her array of other medications. I took this matter to the then Prime Minister Tony Blair, and contacted the *News Letter* newspaper, telling journalist Sandra Chapman the story of my mother's treatment at the assessment unit. I stressed how important it was to stop the use of neuroleptic drugs for Alzheimer's patients. Later, I went on to have a clinical review of my mother's care carried out. The outcome of this was that the assessment unit wasn't a suitable place for my mother to have been treated, but she had been referred there due to the lack of dementia-care facilities in Northern Ireland. The consultant in charge of the unit took early retirement soon after the review was completed.

The process of making the complaint and getting clearance to get the lift passed and installed took months. In that time my mother caught recurrent chest infections and was in and out of hospital for long stays. I eventually got the lift installed, only to be told by one of my siblings that I was 'ruining the property'. I was stunned by this. My father and I were doing all in our power to make life easier for my mother. Dad was deeply saddened when he overheard this exchange.

Mum never got to use the lift. She caught another chest infection in January 2005 and was taken into hospital again. She was still there in March. One afternoon Dad and I went to visit. As we arrived she sat upright in the bed and shouted 'John' to my father. He was amazed; she hadn't known him or said his name for so long. He ran to her, took her into his arms and they clung desperately to each other. 'I love you, I love you, I love you,' she said quickly. It was as though she knew she wouldn't be able to bypass the Alzheimer's monster for long, and needed to get her message across before it claimed her again. My father sobbed, 'Oh Chris, my wee birdie (his pet name for her), I love you, too.'

I watched them in their own world, lost in this incredibly precious moment. Tears flowed down my cheeks. My father's eyes were closed in ecstasy as he held my mother close. He had waited so long for this moment, almost certainly believing he would never hear her say those words to him again or that he would be able to hold her to him. Lord knows what this effort took for Mum, but she was determined that she wasn't leaving this world without telling my father one last time that she loved him and saying goodbye. I felt so proud of her; she had always been a sparky character! For that short time the most important identity my father had ever had – that of her husband – had been reinstated. They were like infatuated teenagers, gazing into each other's eyes. A million conversations seemed to pass between them in one look as a lifetime of love was remembered.

Mum went to sleep later, holding my father's hand and smiling up at him. She never regained consciousness.

Days later, she died. It was both a heartache and a relief. The Alzheimer's nightmare was finally over. Perhaps now I could tentatively begin my life.

As I closed my eyes to go to sleep that night I had the

strangest sensation. It was as though someone was cuddling up behind me, holding me in their arms. I was filled with a feeling of great tranquillity and peace. No one was there. I felt like the house was holding me within its protective embrace.

# It's Better to Wear Out
# Than to Run Out

After Mum's death Steven was a tower of strength. My father claimed he didn't know what we would have done without him. Steven helped us with Mum's funeral arrangements and hurried the builders to get them out of the house.

Mum's GP phoned to offer me her condolences. She had been a great doctor to both Mum and I over the years and I thanked her for all that she had done for my mother. She told me that there was no doubt in her mind that my mother would not have lived as long as she did without the care I had given her. I was grateful to her for saying that.

After Mum's ashes were laid I asked Steven over for dinner. 'What are you doing on the 19th of August?' I asked him.

'Nothing,' he replied, 'Why?'

'We're getting married. I've already booked the church!' I announced.

Nothing was going to stand in our way now.

'Finally!' he beamed and held me close.

Twenty-four years after our first meeting we had a small but lovely wedding, with a princess dress (picked by my father) and all! I was still struggling with panic attacks so I didn't want a big affair. It was difficult not having my mother there. It had only been five months since her death and I felt her absence greatly. Dad walked me down the aisle and cried with every step. He was glad that I was getting married, but upset that my mother wasn't there to see it. As the old saying goes, he wasn't losing a daughter, he was gaining a son.

Our plan had been to buy a lovely luxury apartment at the top of the next street and that I would pop in and out to see Dad daily and to cook his meals. But my father came to me tearfully one night after I told him our wedding plans, and asked me to move

Steven into our family home so that we could all live together. He was terrified of the prospect of living alone, as he had never done so. I was thirty-nine and had lived my life entirely with and for my parents. I had been a carer for twenty years. I dreamed of having my own little home with Steven but, of course, I couldn't walk away from my dad. I adored him and he had just lost the love of his life, while I was about to marry mine. I asked Steven if he would be willing to move in to keep Dad company. It was a big ask, but thankfully he agreed. It didn't seem to matter what terms and conditions I came with; Steven still wanted me and would put up with it all.

As it turned out we all lived happily together. Then I began to feel quite ill. My body felt leaden; I was weepy, nauseous, and exhausted. I'd never felt like this before. My friend suggested I should do a pregnancy test. As I waited on the result I thought it would be just a matter of ruling pregnancy out. But when I looked at the indicator panel, to my amazement, I saw the faintest of pink dots. It was the surprise of my life. Three months after our wedding, at thirty-nine years of age, I discovered I was pregnant! I sat there staring at the dot, deeply shocked but ecstatic. I was going to be a mother.

Steven and Dad were both delighted. Dad had all sorts of plans.

'I can push the pram!' I can help you!' he said.

His future grandchild gave him a new focus. He seemed to fall in love with my child even before it was born.

Our baby made his entrance into the world on our first wedding anniversary, at exactly the same time we had walked down the aisle. I had gone from standing at the altar to lying on the operating table, having an emergency C-section performed, in one year to the minute!

Steven held my hand throughout my operation. Then the doctor showed my baby boy to me. He was wrapped in a blue sheet with his right fist raised in the air and a grumpy expression on his face with one eye closed. He looked like Popeye! I stared curiously at this rather large bundle and hoped desperately that he would like me. We named him Benjamin. He was put onto my chest and as I was wheeled out of surgery I phoned Dad on my mobile and told him he had a grandson. He was chuffed to bits.

My father doted on Ben. They had a special bond. When my father came into the room Ben would break into a smile. Dad was true to his word and mucked in with everything to do with the baby from bathing him to disposing of dirty nappies. Surprisingly, the four of us were a happy, little unit. Steven treated my dad as he did his own father: with respect and affection. I was still suffering from panic attacks and agoraphobia, but I was making progress with conquering it. The stability and love I had found with Steven gave me a new inner strength and I wanted to be the best person I could possibly be for Ben.

Sandra Chapman, the journalist who had run the story about my mother's treatment the year before, had become a good friend after my mother's death. She got in touch to see how I was doing after having the baby. Sandra suggested that writing about my experience as a carer might prove a form of therapy for me and help raise awareness of Alzheimer's disease. As features editor at the *News Letter*, she published my piece about losing my mother to Alzheimer's and the stress suffered by carers of those with dementia. This publication resulted in an appearance on the Stephen Nolan radio programme talking about my experiences as my mother's carer and Alzheimer's disease. Soon I had a weekly column called 'Jackie's World' in the Belfast *News Letter*. Eleven years later I am still writing it. The readers have followed all the ups and downs of my life.

Time passed and my father started to become confused and distant. I watched him making his porridge one morning and observed that he had forgotten how to carry out this simple task. Alarm bells began to ring in my mind, but I didn't want to face the possibility that Dad could have Alzheimer's. He'd always been so fit and vibrant; he had rarely been to a doctor's surgery in his life. But I had to face the truth: Dad wasn't himself. Just like Mum, he wanted to be by my side constantly; he seemed to feel secure when he was with me. This proved a strain on my marriage as my father would stand outside my bedroom door most of the night, or he would simply come in and stand at the bottom of the bed, smiling. Soon my life was all about the care of my father. Luckily, Ben was an incredibly good child. He was pleasant and mild-tempered and seemed to have an old soul. He would hug me reassuringly. Sometimes I felt like he could see inside my heart to all the pain and grief that continually bubbled there.

In December 2008 my father was diagnosed with having 100 percent Alzheimer's. I was told on the telephone a few days before Christmas, after my father had had a brain scan. The monster was back!

'I'm warning you now that this will be a very fast progression,' said the nurse, as kindly as she could. I put down the phone and sat there, stunned. How on earth was I going to cope this time around with a two-year-old child? Obviously, I'd guessed that Dad had some form of dementia but it was easier to deal with before a label was put on it.

The nurse had been right; Dad went downhill very fast. I never got a break between caring for Dad and Ben. I asked my sister if she could help in some way. She said I could take Dad over to her house and leave him with her for lunch on a Sunday while Steven, Ben, and I had a few hours break. I was so grateful!

It started well, we had a few Sundays in a row where we left Dad in her care, but it wasn't always convenient for her. In all, during the course of a year, my sister took Dad on fourteen Sundays. My brother took him on one. I needed a more permanent arrangement, where I could look forward to a break every week. I was desperately in need of regular and reliable help.

Dad's condition was worsening daily, then one afternoon he soiled himself. I think that was one of the most traumatic things I had to deal with in my time as a carer. Practically overnight my father sadly became doubly incontinent.

I went to my GP for help, and was promised a social worker, but waited for months while nothing happened. Then I was asked to talk about Alzheimer's again on the Stephen Nolan show. I told my tale of how I was still waiting for a social worker and was desperately in need of help. Through Nolan's involvement (I could never thank the people on his show enough), days later, a social worker arrived at my door! Her name was Marie, the woman was a saint and an angel rolled into one. I will always be grateful to her for all her efforts; she saved my sanity and my marriage! I had been coping with Dad's double incontinence for almost a year. At the beginning I thought this was the deal breaker – that I would never be able to cope. But when you love someone with all your heart you will do anything for them. I got myself some surgical masks and gloves and contacted the council, who provided me with an extra bin, and Dad and I faced the storm together as always. We soon got over the embarrassment of toileting. I was already showering and washing him each morning, so both our modesties had gone out the window long ago. Marie arranged for a few hours on a Wednesday afternoon where Dad would go to a nearby care home in the afternoon, then come home at teatime. He hated going and after a few visits he escaped and was found wandering down the road. I was so scared of anything happening to him I wouldn't let him go anywhere after that and, with his double incontinence problem, there was no question of any of my siblings looking after him.

Dad was becoming increasingly unsteady on his feet and one morning he stumbled over in the shower. I tried my best to help him up but ended up having to get into the shower with him, get behind him with my hands beneath his armpits, lift him, and guide him out. I was fully clothed and soaking wet. I could hear that Ben had woken up, put Dad in a commode chair in the bathroom wrapped in a robe and ran to get to Ben only to slip on the bathroom floor. I began to sob uncontrollably. I just lay there. I didn't know how much more I could take. Then I felt my father's hand on my head. I looked up into his face; he could no longer speak but the look he gave me was one of heartfelt sorrow. We may as well have both had Alzheimer's because it had claimed my life almost as much as it had claimed his.

After this, Marie stepped in and began putting what she could in place for me. I hadn't wanted care assistants in because of my experience with my mother. Also I didn't want to feel like we were living in a care home. I was trying to keep my marriage from falling apart. We lived and breathed Dad's care, but I had reached a stage where I could no longer cope with all of Dad's care by myself.

Two care assistants would visit in the morning to get Dad up and wash and dress him. I only had them on weekday mornings and saw to Dad myself at the weekends when Steven was able to look after Ben. I did this to try and keep some semblance of normality as a family during weekends, without crack-of-dawn calls from care assistants. The carers came in the evening, too, to put Dad to bed. They also visited once at lunchtime to take him to the loo, though obviously I still had to toilet Dad the rest of the time myself. They were very kind girls and I liked them very much, but even they could see I was struggling to cope with Dad, along with a toddler, full-time. I had no privacy, no real time to myself. Steven, Ben, and I were able to get a few hours out on a Sunday when a carer from an agency would come to sit with Dad but, frankly, I was still struggling. I went out but, battling with my panic, I always had to have Steven within touching distance and couldn't go anywhere on my own. I was having home visits from a CBT therapist who was helping me overcome my anxiety problems. He told me that I had the worst case of burnout he'd ever seen, and refused to see me again until I arranged respite care for a break for myself. He said until I got some proper rest it was pointless to carry on taking my money as nothing would change. I thought this was terribly harsh and was annoyed with him. The care assistants began to urge me to get a break, too, as did Marie. They all told me that it would be impossible to keep up this level of care for my father, along with a raising a toddler, not to mention the effect constantly having a demented parent by your side can have on a marriage. The therapist, the care assistants, and Marie were all right. Emotionally, mentally, and physically, I was a mess but, like many carers, I was of the belief that it was better to wear out than to run out.

Things really disintegrated when I caught a nasty virus. I was in the kitchen trying to make lunch for Dad and Ben, when my legs gave way beneath me, and I slid to the floor. I just lay there looking at my father and my boy. I had reached the end of my rope.

Later I rang Marie and begged her for help. She said I needed emergency respite immediately. She got a place for my father the next day, just for a week or two, until I got over my virus, she said.

The next day will live in my memory as the saddest, most

traumatic day of my life. I didn't know how to tell my father that he would be going to stay elsewhere for a while. I had packed his bag and lay awake all night sobbing my heart out. In all my life, my father and I had never been apart for more than a matter of days. I felt I was letting him down and was ashamed of myself for having to take this course of action. I felt intense guilt, too.

Special transport had been arranged to collect Dad. I had explained as best I could to him what was happening. As he passed me at the front door he put his hand on my shoulder and gave me a reassuring pat and a look of sympathy, as though he understood I had no choice. I couldn't even hug him because I would have become hysterical and not been able to let him go. When he left I sobbed for hours. I knew when he had walked out the door that everything had changed. He was gone from me in so many ways.

I gradually built up my strength. I wanted to go down every day to visit Dad, but Marie said it would only unsettle him and I needed a proper break. After two weeks I was ready to take Dad home, but Marie dissuaded me. I went to visit and my father seemed settled. He had absolutely no idea who I was. Weeks passed and, for the first time in years, I felt what it was like to have a life of my own. It was liberating but difficult to adjust. I had never been alone, and being in the house all day with just my toddler while my husband was at work seemed daunting. For the first time in my life I was living without a parental presence. I was forty-three years old! I began to listen to music again, something I hadn't done for so long. I would play Gordon Haskell's album *Harry's Bar* constantly, particularly the song 'Al Capone'; there was something about his voice and the rhythm of the music in this song that seemed to reach inside and soothe me. I didn't feel quite so alone with Gordon playing in the background; he was like musical diazepam!

My father's Alzheimer's continued to progress and I knew in my heart that I couldn't possibly take care of him at home again. My son was getting ready to go to pre-school; I was still battling my panic and didn't drive, so I would have to take Ben to nursery in a taxi, as I couldn't walk there with my agoraphobia. If I took Dad out of the care home, I would have to take him with me on the school runs as I couldn't leave him alone. The practicalities of taking Dad and Ben out twice a day together in a taxi, while battling my panic attacks, didn't bear thinking about.

Finally, Dad became a permanent resident at the home. Steven, Ben and I visited religiously but the house felt empty and huge with him gone; I think it missed him as much as I did.

Watching my father's deterioration as Alzheimer's devoured him was torturous. I felt so helpless and hopeless. Over time the disease stripped my father of everything: from his speech and mobility, to his ability to swallow food. He had no idea who I was. I doubt he even knew who he was. My father became emaciated; he looked dreadful and began to fall prey to numerous infections. Then began the inevitable round of ambulance dashes and hospital admittances, just as it had with my mother.

Hospital stays for an Alzheimer's sufferer are nothing short of horrendous. My father couldn't communicate and, with a small child to care for, I couldn't be with him all the time. Dad was in hospital during a time of extreme weather conditions. Snow was deep on the ground, temperatures plummeted. When he was thought fit enough to go back to the care home, he was taken in an ambulance late at night. The staff rang me to tell me the very distressing news that he had been sent out of hospital in freezing temperatures wearing just a pyjama top and a pair of incontinence pants with not even a blanket around his freezing legs. The care assistant, who was very fond of my father, was terribly distressed when telling me this. I wrote a letter of complaint immediately to the hospital trust. I was furious that my father had been treated in such a cruel and undignified manner. I received a letter of apology back from the trust, ensuring me this would never happen again. Six weeks later it did! My father was again sent out of a different hospital in an ambulance in freezing weather wearing just a nappy and a pyjama top. Not even a blanket had been thrown over his legs on either occasion to cover his modesty or keep him warm. Would the staff who did this want their own loved ones treated in this way?

The problem with this vile disease is that a person with Alzheimer's is regarded by many as persona non grata. When my father was himself he could charm the birds out of the trees; people, often strangers, would go out of their way to help him in any way they could, because when they were on the receiving end of his charm, he made them feel good about themselves. But when my father was no longer able to communicate, his vulnerability was taken advantage of. He wasn't capable of using his charm so there was nothing to gain from showing him kindness. It is terrifying and heart-breaking the way those with Alzheimer's are sometimes treated. Even staff in some care homes can be horrifyingly cruel, as has been recently highlighted in the media. And there will always be those within families who turn a blind eye to those who suffer with this disease because it evokes uncomfortable feelings within them that they would rather not have to face.

I wrote to the trust again the second time my father was discharged in a state of undress and received a response apologising and informing me, 'The trust needs to further learn and develop an understanding of the meaning of dementia.'

Isn't hospital the one place where the needs of those who are ill should be understood?

During the time my father was at the care home, one of the assistants phoned me and asked if my father had ever played the piano? I said Dad had once been a professional musician with his own orchestra, that's how he met my mother back in the dancehall days. On enquiring why she'd asked, she replied my father had been receiving music therapy at the home and had begun to mime playing the piano, while one particular song caused tears to flow down his face.

The song was 'Moonlight Serenade'; it had been my parents' special love song. To this day I cannot hear it played without breaking down. Music had always been one of my father's passions and it was clearly able to unlock the memory box inside his mind that contained my mother. I put down the phone and sobbed at the thought of him still being able to recall and miss my mother. All night I couldn't get Dad's musical memory out of my head, until a mad idea came to me. Perhaps I could ask celebrities if there was a certain song that evoked a special memory for them and put them into a book in aid of the Alzheimer's Society. The first publisher I went to, Accent Press, loved the idea and within months two-hundred-and-sixteen celebrities, including two prime ministers, had donated memories along with messages of support from the Dalai Lama, Prince Charles and Prince William. The book; *They Can't Take That Away From Me*, was published with one hundred percent of my royalties going to the Alzheimer's Society. It was talked about on the television, written about in magazines and newspapers, and discussed on the radio. Something worthwhile had come out of this Alzheimer's nightmare after all! Mum and Dad would have loved it, had they known a book about their love story had been published with the help of lots of famous people. It was my tribute to them and their love for each other.

Dad's condition continued to worsen; he was a husk of himself. He simply lay on the bed, slowly starving to death. When he had been in hospital the doctors had asked if peg-feeding might be an option. I was horrified by this and thankfully it wasn't discussed further. My father was in such a dreadful state that the only thing I wanted for him was death. He had suffered for so long that he deserved some peace. It was soon to come.

The nurse from the care home phoned me one Saturday afternoon, telling me Dad was in a bad way. I knew things were coming to a head. By this stage my agoraphobia had been brought under control with the help of hypnotherapy, reflexology, and herbal supplements.

I went to my father and stayed the whole day with him, waiting for the doctor. I called my siblings to let them know Dad was very ill. We had been at this point so many times in the past few months, being told that Dad was at death's door, only to see him pulled back from the brink. I didn't know what to expect.

It was a really wet, dark day. I sat with my father holding his hand as he lay in bed. I put on some Frank Sinatra for him; I had brought down all his favourite music weeks before and would often play him tunes. It made him smile. Then 'My Way' came on. I jumped up and turned the music off. I couldn't cope with listening to Sinatra's words. I sat in silence with my father as he dozed, waiting for the doctor. Hours passed. I watched the rain trickle down the windowpanes and the raindrops drip from the leaves on the trees outside, as though they were crying. It reminded me of an old song by Donovan that I loved called

'Catch the Wind'. I began to sing it to my father as he slept. It was odd to hear my voice breaking the silence in the room.

Someone cleared their voice behind me. A doctor had finally arrived, I felt a bit daft sitting there, warbling out of tune, my face awash. The nurse from the care home joined him. The doctor examined my father, there was much hushed whispering, then the nurse smiled sympathetically at me.

'Your father is very ill …' the doctor began,

'How much longer?' I asked, interrupting him.

He was a little taken aback by my outburst.

'Please, doctor, I have to know.'

He nodded his head understandingly.

'We are talking a matter of days,' he said putting a reassuring hand on my shoulder.

'Thank you,' I said perfectly calmly. There were no more tears, I was very calm. I phoned my siblings and let them know what the doctor had said. I sat for some time with Dad, thinking of my entire lifetime spent with him, trying to come to terms with the fact that this was the end of our story. Then I returned to the house that had once been my father's home. Memories of him came out to greet me from every room. I was in a sort of daze. I felt emotionally and physically exhausted with the effort that this long-running death watch had taken out of me; it had been going on for months. Some days I was prepared for him to go, others I just wanted one more day with him.

Six days after the doctor's pronouncement my father was still surviving. I went to see him. He was sitting up in bed, drifting in and out of sleep. I closed the door and climbed on the bed beside him. I snuggled up to him and put my head on his shoulder. He smiled. And there we lay in absolute silence. I remembered all our times together. On Ballywalter beach when I would get up on a wall and walk along holding his hand, I thought I was great because I felt tall and thought people would think I was a grown-up, walking along with my daddy. I recalled him teaching me to swim and our weekly trips to church every Sunday, just the two of us together, for thirty-plus years we attended. I remembered him dropping me off on my first day at grammar school; I stopped to look over my shoulder at him waiting in the car, before entering nervously through those big school gates. He gave me a reassuring smile as he watched me go in. I remembered how he would always leave a light on for me when I went out for the night. It was partly for my safety and partly so that he would know when I had returned home if the light was turned off. I knew he didn't sleep until I was safely back in the house.

I didn't cry. I just lay there with Dad and enjoyed feeling him beside me, knowing I must savour every second. Then I felt a spiritual presence in the room, one of great peace and serenity; something or someone not of this world had joined us, but I wasn't afraid. Dad was preparing to leave this world. I wrapped my arms around my father and held him tight. I felt in my heart that this was goodbye, that this could be the last embrace.

'I love you, Daddy, forever and ever,' I whispered in his ear.

That evening I found it hard to leave him. When I got off the bed and walked to the door, the atmosphere felt thick and heavy to move through. Every action had a poignancy, as though I was doing it all for the last time. I stopped at the door, my hand on the handle, then turned back to look at him in the bed asleep.

'Leave a light on in heaven for me, Daddy,' I said softly, then exited with a stomach filled with grief.

It was the last time I saw my father alive; he died the following day before I could reach him.

The evening of his death I lay alone in bed and felt the same warm invisible embrace I had experienced on the night of my mother's death, as though someone was holding me tight. Was it the spirit of the house comforting me, that same presence I have felt so many times when I'm alone? Whatever or whoever it was, it felt very real; the sensation helped me get through the first night in this new world where my father no longer existed.

# You've Come a Long Way Baby

As the stranger stood at the door lost in his memories, I too was immersed in my history. Past events had unfolded like a mental movie. I had seen all the faces that I loved and precious times flicker across the cinema screen in my mind. We had been standing in the doorway for almost half an hour communicating little to each other but reliving lifetimes in our heads. I still wasn't going to let him in. A tiny part of me was scared in case 'the presence' left with him. It wasn't lost on me that we were standing in the same doorway that he left by almost fifty years ago and I had entered in my mother's arms on his departure. It was a portal to our parents, our childhoods, our histories.

Our childhood homes can leave deep imprints on our souls, they become part of our identity. My father left the house to me in his will, no doubt to compensate for asking me to forgo having a house of my own and stay with him when I married. He was not going to leave me homeless on his death. My father's last will and testament caused an irreparable breakdown in my relationship with my siblings. They tried to contest the will by claiming diminished mental capacity on my father's part and, much to my disgust and heartbreak, undue influence on mine.

My father had offered to put the house into my name when I got married and I refused to let him do so. I wanted him to know I was there because I loved him; there was no price, conditions or clauses involved for me to stay with my father when he needed me. Nor did I want him to feel he was no longer king of his own castle.

The house that built me, broke me down, stripped me of an entire family, gave me a new one and rebuilt me.

Research has revealed that we are most likely to revisit the childhood home we were raised in between the ages of five and twelve, because these are our most formative years. The urge usually comes when we are going through a crisis or a problem and feel the need to reflect on our past, to try perhaps to figure out why we have made the life choices we made.

I couldn't blame the former resident for returning. I could feel his sadness, his desperation to go back, to recreate what had once been his perfect reality; it was there for me, too! We both looked back on our childhood years with wonder. It was a time when parents were healthy and families were whole. Becoming an adult orphan brings with it a melancholy that seems to take residence in your soul. It brings a feeling of aloneness that no other relationship can ever really replace. Grief complicates and changes us. The loss becomes an eternal missing and everything connected with our loved ones becomes sacred and reverent. The man was searching for his younger self, wrapped in the security of childhood, complete with a set of protective parents. He felt in his heart that a trace of his parents still remained here. Perhaps it does, along with particles of souls belonging to all the other late former residents of the house, including the mother and the soldier whose letters had been found in the attic.

'Has it been a happy home?' he asked, his eyes beginning to mist.

'Yes,' I affirmed fervently, swallowing back a ball of emotion, because despite and even sometimes during the Alzheimer's years, it had been, and still was a happy home.

'It was for me, too', he concluded, wiping his eyes with the big cotton hankie he'd produced from his trouser pocket.

'I'm glad I came,' he said turning to go. 'I feel comforted'.

And with that we said tearful goodbyes. It was as though the house had given him a sympathetic hug, then thrown its reassuring arm around me.

I closed the door and thought about our encounter, then I rushed to tear something off the wall I wanted him to have. By the time I got outside he was gone. I knew nothing about him except that his name was Mr Moffat and that he lived in New Zealand. Maybe someday I will track him down and be able to pass on my gift. It was a poem that I wrote for my parents' fiftieth wedding anniversary entitled 'Waterloo', the name the house has always held, even the ghost hunter had called it that. It was written pre-Alzheimer's in 1997, yet seemed so poignant now. It was as though I had written it in anticipation of his coming. I had the poem framed for my parents. Perhaps when I move from the house, I shall leave the poem in situ for the next residents, to let them know just how special and much loved this home has been.

# WATERLOO

This house has heard much laughter
It's had its share of tears
It's welcomed many strangers
Through the ceaseless flow of years.
Each corner houses memories
Of lives that have passed through
It's comforted some troubled hearts
And helped the sun shine through.
There's serenity in being here
A shelter in life's storms
The atmosphere enfolds you
Keeps you safe and warm.

Waterloo's seen weddings, births, success
Sad times are few
It also has its secrets
More than one or two!
It holds a family history
Tight within its arms
Seduces those who enter
With homely winning charms
For the children who were raised here
No matter where we roam
Our hearts remain embedded
In this loving family home.

The man's visit had a lasting effect on me. I couldn't get his
melancholy search for memories out my head. Then strangely I
heard a song on the radio called 'The House That Built Me',
which spookily echoed the experience of my unexpected visitor.
The song described a woman revisiting her childhood home,
having felt she had lost her way in the world since leaving it, and
that perhaps coming to the house again could heal the

brokenness she felt inside. It was then that the idea came to me; perhaps I could create another book to help raise awareness and funds for the Alzheimer's Society, again giving the charity 100 percent of the royalties. So I asked people to donate memories of their childhood homes to help those who have lost their memories through Alzheimer's. Many well-known people kindly agreed. They wrote about their childhood homes with affection. It was clear these memories were precious. It wasn't the material things that were remembered by the contributors with any great fondness, it was the love that lived there and the wonderful simplicity of life as a child that they cherished and eternally missed.

# List of Contributors

*With Special Thanks to*

Anne Bennett
Alan Titchmarsh MBE DL
Amanda Lamb
Amelia Bullmore
Ann Widdecombe DSG
Anne Atkins
Anne Nolan
Aykut Hilmi
Bel Mooney
Bill Oddie OBE
Bobby Ball
Carey Mulligan
Carl Fogarty MBE
Christina Jones
Dame Mary Peters CH DBE
Daniel Brocklebank
David Hamilton
Debbie McGee
Deborah Moggach
Diane Keen
Don Warrington MBE
Dr Miriam Stoppard OBE
Ed Balls
Edwina Currie
Fearne Cotton

# LIST OF CONTRIBUTORS

*With Special Thanks to*

FELICITY KENDAL CBE
FENELLA FIELDING
GEMMA JONES
GORDON HASKELL
JANE FALLON
JANE MCDONALD
JEFFREY HOLLAND
JILL MANSELL
JO BRAND
JO WOOD
JULIE PEASGOOD
KACEY AINSWORTH
KIM WILDE
KOO STARK
LEMBIT OPIK
LISA JEWELL
LIZ FRASER
LORRAINE KELLY OBE
MARC BAYLIS
MARGARET JAMES
MICHELLE GAYLE
MILLY JOHNSON
NEIL SEDAKA
NERYS HUGHES
NICHOLAS PARSONS CBE

# LIST OF CONTRIBUTORS

*With Special Thanks to*

NICOLA STEPHENSON
NIGEL HAVERS
PAULA LANE
R. J. ELLORY
RICK GUARD
ROWAN COLEMAN
RUTH BADGER
SAMANTHA GILES
SANDRA CHAPMAN
SANJEEV BHASKAR OBE
SHANE RICHIE
SIMON BATES
SIMON WILLIAMS
SINEAD MORIARTY
SIR TONY ROBINSON
SUE MOORCROFT
TRACIE BENNETT
TRACY-ANN OBERMAN
TRISHA ASHLEY
VERITY RUSHWORTH
YASMIN ALIBHAI-BROWN

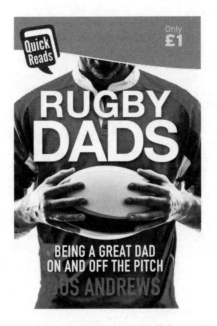

Being a great dad - on and off the pitch.

Fatherhood is an underrated skill. Many fall into it almost by accident. But having done so, they become accidental role models for the next generation.

When that father and role model is a dad who has made his name in rugby, how difficult is it for sons and daughters to follow in his boots and make their own mark? And how do rugby players themselves cope with the pressures of the game, and looking after their little ones?

With personal, family stories from several generations of rugby players and their children, along with tips on how to deal with the stresses and strains of a competitive, strenuous job and family life, this is a rugby book with a difference.

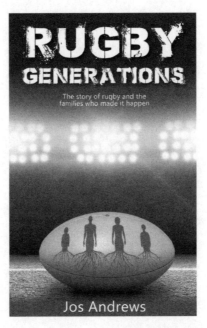

Being a great dad - on and off the pitch

Fatherhood is an underrated skill. Many fall into it almost by accident. But having done so, they become accidental role models for the next generation.

When that father and role model is a dad who has made his name in rugby, how difficult is it for sons and daughters to follow in his boots and make their own mark? And how do rugby players themselves cope with the pressures of the game, and looking after their little ones?

With personal, family stories from several generations of rugby players and their children, along with tips on how to deal with the stresses and strains of a competitive, strenuous job and family life, this is a rugby book with a difference.